IT HAS A NAME!

How To Keep Control Freaks & Other Unhealthy Narcissists From Ruining Your Life.

EA DEUBLE

ASHEHAM PRESS

ASHEHAM PRESS 2010

First Asheham Press trade print edition 2010
PRINTED IN THE UNITED STATES OF AMERICA.

For information, please contact:
ASHEHAM PRESS 5305 WARING ROAD
SAN DIEGO, CA 92120.

ISBN 0-982724829

To Joanna

"It is not our purpose to become each other; it is to recognize each other, to learn to see the other and honor him for what he is."

Hermann Hesse

DISCLAIMER

This book is about my own life experience and the research I conducted. I am not a doctor, psychiatrist, psychologist or sociologist. I make no such claim and am not offering professional counseling or legal advice. I am simply a person who has experienced the damage done first hand from encounters with close family members, friends, co-workers and partners who are unhealthy narcissists. The reader must make their own decisions and come to their own conclusions as to what they are dealing with and how to proceed in their life. For more information on the subject matter covered in this book, I recommend many books and resources by experts and theorists which contain valuable information.

ACKNOWLEDGEMENTS

I wish to thank Joanna Ashmun whose information about unhealthy narcissism helped put me on the path to find answers to questions that had long plagued me about relationship dysfunction. I am forever grateful. I also wish to thank my friends, Doreen, Des and Linda, who listened to me while I struggled in trying to understand the nature of what I had experienced and discovered. Thanks to my life partner, Rosie, who has endured many days of introspection and frustration yet urged me on to complete this book and claim my private triumph, now public. And finally, thanks to Ann Bradley for her contribution to the book and her support. You all have made a positive difference in my life.

Forward   v

Introduction – Let's Begin   viii

1. In Through the Out Door   1

2. Pattern Behavior   22

3. It Takes Two   39

4. Get Out and Stay Out   48

5. What is Abuse?   69

6. Taking Action   80

7. Black & White Thinking   93

8. N-Marriages and Divorce   101

9. Celebrity Narcissism   106

10. Criminal Narcissists & Sociopaths   110

11. Collective Narcissism & Our Future 116

12. Well-Being   139

Afterward   142

My Teachers & Selected Reading   145

Resources for Further Reading   147

Web Resources   151

FORWARD

After having experienced a very distasteful encounter a few years ago with someone I thought to be charming, energetic, and confident, but in fact used their charm to be manipulative, deceptive, and soul killing, I was determined to find out why they were behaving in such a way towards me. My discovery on April 14, 2007 after reading an online description of unhealthy narcissism led me to write in my journal, *it has a name.* Suddenly many things fell into place regarding the root of the dysfunctional nature of my own family and of this, and other relationships, gone awry that I had experienced in my life. On that day I committed myself to one year of finding out as much as I could about the subject of narcissism and the related problems of unhealthy narcissism and NPD, Narcissistic Personality Disorder. Every day for a year I conducted research by reading books and articles by experts on the subject. The following year I began compiling all my notes, and now nearly three years later I have written this book as a result of my journey of discovery.

I hope this book will be an aid to help others recognize the dynamic of unhealthy narcissism that may be playing out in their lives. Not only is there information to help better understand what unhealthy narcissism is, but I also suggest ways to help recover and heal from the damage done when we trust, love, or work for an unhealthy narcissist. My goal is to help others lead a more productive, happier, and healthier life.

This book is a little psychology, a little philosophy, a little sociology, and a little bit of my life experience all rolled into one and expressed through my opinions. As I stated, I studied the subject of unhealthy narcissism for one solid year, a year spent everyday reading and researching the subject and addressing many deep, personal issues. I want you to know it can be emotionally draining and upsetting when you first come to realize that people who you thought loved and cared about you, in fact were using you and manipulating you to satisfy their own very unhealthy narcissistic needs.

Take it slow. Examine what you have been through. This is not a test or judgment about your behavior. You have been deceived and manipulated. You may feel angry, frustrated, hurt, and maybe confused when the subject fully comes to light. You should not be ashamed. You were a target and are not alone in your ignorance of this disorder. Rest assured, many people do not know, if ever, that they were under the control of an unhealthy narcissist. They simply felt bad or guilty or depressed about a relationship gone awry and too often thinking it was their fault for the failure. But for many others, it is all too clear when the person they loved, cared for, or worked for was abusive and manipulative and caused them great personal harm.

My first healing comment to you is: forgive yourself. You were used and abused and treated like an object. No one deserves to be treated like an object.

No one deserves to be disrespected, or diminished, or deceived.

Personal forgiveness can clear the way in your life for you to go on, to make forward progress from the negative place you find yourself. Like clearing a path overgrown with bushes and weeds, you will clear away the overgrown feelings of guilt, hurt, frustration, and self-doubt. Forgiveness will help you to the next stage – awareness and mindfulness. And from there, healing, recovering your dignity, and regaining your sense of self-worth.

INTRODUCTION

Let's Begin

How did I know something was amiss? My own background informed me. Mine was one where I had a controlling, verbally abusive, emotionally absent alcoholic father and a perfectionist, controlling, passive-aggressive mother. What I have come to understand is that not only did they both exhibit unhealthy narcissistic behavior, but upon closer examination, their behavior revealed typical controlling traits. Someone like me who was brought up by this type parent is literally attracted to, and attracts these kinds of people into their life. Why? Because we are familiar with them as they were our archetype, our role model for all other adult relationships, and this sets us up for future engagements with people just like them.

What happened for me was I had a moment of clarity. I finally saw through the unconscious manipulation of an unhealthy narcissist in such a way to ask the question, why were they treating me this way? Why, when I had been a giving and caring person did this person harm me?

Now, these probing questions did not come out of some void. I have been doing what I call my "work", my psychological and emotional work of healing and self-actualization, since I was in high-school in the 60s. During this time I was living with my alcoholic father after my parents divorced a few years earlier. As a child I had always been very curious about life in general taking an early interest in history and the lives of real people. After my parents divorced I was very open to discovering new ways of thinking and living in the world - ways that were counter to the chaos and hurt that existed in my dysfunctional family. Fostering my own individual development, I began reading books by Hermann Hesse when I was 16. Books like *Demian, Siddhartha,* and *Journey to the East* helped put me on the path to self-discovery and led me to my initial studies of psychoanalysis, psychology, and eastern philosophy.

The significance of finding a kindred spirit cannot be stressed enough. This kind of validation and affirmation is welcome to an abused person. The key was I knew there were other, better and healthier ways of thinking, living and being outside my family experience and I actively pursued this knowledge. I wanted to be free of the dysfunction. And while I was open to other ways of thinking, it was not until I came to understand through someone else's experience, and learning about their journey of self-discovery, how I could go about claiming a different life – how I could claim my authentic self and pursue a new life. It was through Hesse and his description of his childhood problems and how he struggled with his self-development (expressed in his book *Demian),* that I was able to find a way out of my own life circumstance and set about my life path. Hesse helped create a vital connection for me with life outside and beyond the abusive family environment.

The book *Demian* is about a young boy, Emil Sinclair, who is a victim of bullying from another older schoolmate – Franz Kromer. The bully enslaves Emil through blackmail. But Emil is also enslaved in his mind by religious values indoctrinated by his parents – values he comes to find have no real power to help protect him in the real world, the world outside his family life. Emil's saving grace is through a powerful friendship with another young boy, Max Demian, who exudes inner strength, intelligence, empathy and confidence. Through a series of encounters between the two boys Max eventually intervenes to help free Emil from the blackmailing bully. From that point on, Emil begins his journey of self-discovery and recovery. In the process, Demian challenges Emil's to question his way of thinking and his religious values. Emil starts to see through the inherent weakness of dogmatic thought and that there are other ways of thinking, behaving and being in the world.

What is important to understand is that the role of Demian is one of counselor, friend, and new archetype. He represents light. His role is crucial in Emil's life to help him recover his dignity and escape the darkness of doubt that had surrounded his feelings of self. Demian helps Emil emerge from the self-doubt which had plagued him as a bullied victim. The friendship between Emil and Demian extends into young adulthood and ends at the onset of World War I. Demian's last words to Emil as he lay dying from wounds he has suffered are the critical life lesson Hesse has for victims of abuse: "Perhaps you will need me again sometime, against Kromer or something. If you call me then I won't come crudely, on horseback or train. You'll have to listen within yourself, and then you will notice that I am within you."

I am within you. Demian reassures Emil that the qualities he saw in him, Emil now possesses himself to deal with whatever comes his way. The message found in *Demian* is one of finding our true self and our inner hero – even if that means being an anti-hero and rejecting social norms and religious dogma. It is about claiming our self-worth and right to live an authentic life free from oppression and manipulation. For Hesse, *Demian* was the beginning of a lifelong theme which would appear in many of his books: the conflict between the world of light (the secret life of family and related beliefs and values) and the outside world (of illusion and darkness) and the path that lay in between of self-realization. What we come to understand is within each world lies truth and light - deception and darkness. The path is one we all tread in one way or another. I still keep this book by my bedside as it has played - and continues to play - a pivotal role in my life.

Lucky for me in my teen years it was the 60s and my subsequent rebellion, like so many others of my generation, served me well. My goal was to break free from the verbal abuse and emotional bullying of my father. In my English literature class I was introduced to Hesse which then led me to other insightful authors, namely Carl Jung and Erich Fromm. My book shelves still hold the many books from those days: B.F Skinner, Erich Fromm, Rollo May, Abraham Maslow, Jung, and Hesse. Through them I became a student of *ontology*, known as the study of being. In Maslow, I found and embraced the theory of *self-actualization* which profoundly changed my life. I came to know the *Shadow self* as described by Jung. I expanded my understanding of world religions and philosophies and belief systems. And through it all I effectively reintroduced myself to my self: this is who you are – and I liked what I found. I continued my new life path by adopting new ways of believing and creating my own value system. I practiced Yoga and developed my own kind of philosophy. I synthesized what I had learned to form my own worldview. While Yoga is a discipline, it lent itself to a more flexible way of thinking as I was able to develop the art of mindfulness through meditation. At the end of this book is a section with a list of authors who I call, *My Teachers*. I know each person has their own values and worldview, but I encourage the reader to sample their readings.

As with all people though, I have had to actually live my life – life outside research, study, and devotion. The daily grind and grit of life is demanded of each person and accordingly I have experienced a mixture of adventures, triumphs, struggles and failures. In looking back at failed or troubled relationships I have tried to judge each one separately. This last encounter which prompted the writing of this book began with some hard questions: Was this happening due to some old victim behavior of mine? And even though I knew the signs of abuse, how did I become entrapped again? The frustration and hurt from my experience with what I came to realize as a master manipulator caused me to say to myself, I thought I was beyond all that – what is going here? How did I allow this to happen? The quest to know the answers has propelled my life in a new direction. It is the period beneath the exclamation mark. It Has A Name!

What I Have Discovered

The 'It' in It Has A Name, is *unhealthy narcissism*. In my case it is the root of abusive behavior whereby persons with an unhealthy sense of self, (i.e. grandiose sense of self-importance, incessant need for admiration, lack of empathy, arrested emotions, and overblown sense of entitlement), manipulate others for their own needs – that of attention and domination.

After exhaustive research my own conclusion is the underpinnings of unhealthy narcissism are expressed in tangent with conclusions made by someone I have studied for over four decades, the noted psychologist, Carl Jung. Jung believed our self is the unity and totality of the personality. Narcissism is our sense of self. Our early childhood development can result in either a healthy whole self, or an unhealthy fragmented self. If, in our early infant years we receive healthy mirroring, support, love, nurturing, empathy and understanding, our core self will emerge in a healthy way setting us on the path to what Jung labeled *individuation*. But, if we are lacking in those elements from our caretakers and instead are denied healthy mirroring, warmth and caring, and our concerns are ignored, sidelined and diminished, our fragile developing self will become fragmented and individuation is not only interrupted, but impaired. Our personal identity is tied to proper individuation, meaning how we develop into an autonomous being with a healthy sense of self. When inherent needs are not met early on, the developing child will compensate. In the yearning for wholeness, a child will adapt his personality to the conditions surrounding them. For the child who lacks vital healthy support, their personality will become maladapted, resulting in an unhealthy sense of sense, i.e. unhealthy narcissism.

"Individuation: In developmental psychology - particularly analytical psychology - individuation is the process through which a person becomes his/her 'true self'. Hence it is the process whereby the innate elements of personality; the different experiences of a person's life and the different aspects and components of the immature psyche become integrated over time into a well-functioning whole. Individuation might thus be summarized as the stabilizing of the personality."

Source: Wikipedia, Individuation

It is important to note that it is not a black and white proposition. Unhealthy narcissism operates on a sliding scale from people who exhibit some traits who are mildly controlling, to control freaks, to people who exhibit narcissistic behavior, to full blown narcissistic personality disorder, with malignant narcissism (as seen in sociopaths), on the most extreme end. This is an important point to understand so we refrain from labeling someone as NPD when perhaps they are simply controlling personalities. That does not excuse controlling behavior, but we must keep our assessments in check with reality and not some exaggerated projection that carries pejorative connotations.

While Jung answers many questions about the self, I found a fuller explanation lay with Austrian-born American psychoanalyst, Heinz Kohut, the father of Self Psychology. Together, Jung's and Kohut's complementary theories have answered for me what I needed to understand as to the why's and how's of unhealthy narcissism. They have provided the nitty-gritty - the machinations of maladapted personality development. Ironically, it was not until the last chapter of this book was written that I stumbled upon the 1985 book, *Individuation and Narcissism: the Psychology of Self in Jung and Kohut, by Mario Jacoby.* It was a welcome and coincidental affirmation of my own conclusions distilled in these two men's theories. Jacoby's findings reinforced my view that narcissism has healthy and unhealthy aspects and is a result of early childhood development.

While persons with healthy narcissism have a positive sense of self, (healthy integration of self-esteem, self-image, and self-worth), the person with unhealthy narcissism is the opposite with a negative sense of self, (fragmented self-image, low self-esteem, and diminished self-worth), they are therefore compelled to feed their weak self-esteem through self-centered behavior and a fallacious high regard for themselves – meaning, they create a grandiose sense of self.

Early childhood experiences of abuse, neglect, strong-parenting, under-appreciation or over-the-top expectations, etc., have a profound negative effect on the developing psyche. Thus, unhealthy narcissism is overcompensation for inferiority within one's psyche. To be sure, let's be clear: not all people who exhibit unhealthy narcissism are monsters or sociopaths; some are even shy, yet controlling through passive-aggression. But the question we must ask is how do you know the depth of their disorder? Unfortunately, it is by our experience with them.

Let's understand a little more about what we are dealing with by looking at some expert research based on the findings of Heinz Kohut. First off, narcissism is a function of our psyche and as such is a necessary aspect in the development of the human mind and sense of self. The term, *he or she is a narcissist*, is more a description of negative behavior (denoting vanity, conceit, egotism or simple selfishness), versus the actual definition and description of the psychological personality disorder. The two, while seemingly similar, are different. While some people are arrogant, not all arrogant people are unhealthy narcissists.

Additionally, there is ASN, or Acquired Situational Narcissism, "*a form of narcissism that develops in late adolescence or adulthood, brought on by wealth, fame and the other trappings of celebrity. ASN differs from conventional narcissism in that it develops after childhood and is triggered and supported by the celebrity-obsessed society: fans, assistants and tabloid media all play into the idea that the person really is vastly more important than other people, triggering a narcissistic problem that might have been only a tendency, or latent, and helping it to become a full-blown personality disorder."*

"In its presentation and symptoms, it is indistinguishable from narcissistic personality disorder, differing only in its late onset and its support by large numbers of others. The person with ASN may suffer from unstable relationships, substance abuse and erratic behavior. "

Source: Wikipedia, Acquired Situational Narcissism

So, let's break it down. What is 'it'? Unhealthy Narcissism is love of ones' self and refers to a set of personality and character traits whereby a person is completely consumed with self-admiration, self-centeredness and self-regard. *Love,* as it is used in this case, means self-involvement versus affectionate or caring behavior that most of us think of when we think of love. It is attention turned inward to keep the focus on the false-self to help the shaky fragmented personality cope. Ironically, they are unsure of themselves, but display high levels of confidence to compensate. (The false-self is based on the grandiose-self that first occurs in early childhood development).

What we find is the unhealthy narcissist demands from others high regard, constant admiration, subordination, and to be the center of attention without any regard for others. This kind of selfish behavior goes far beyond conceit, or arrogance, or egoism, although all of those are in play at some level. What is perhaps the most important thing to understand is unhealthy narcissism is a pervasive pattern of behavior that exacts a high toll on others who interact with them. Reason being is they are competitive and highly focused on self-gratification – usually at the expense of others.

Healthy narcissistic traits on the other hand imply knowing one's limitations, having good boundaries, respecting others, having a realistic sense of self-worth, and taking enjoyment in one's own actions. These healthy traits are gained through empathic positive mirroring and support from the parent or caretaker.

Aside from positive mirroring, there are other needs of the developing child that need to be met as well to insure healthy development: Acknowledgment (meaning accepting the person for who they are based in reality and not a projection by the parent); Echoing (repeating back what the child has said for positive reinforcement), Understanding and sympathy (both also strengthening elements for the developing empathy and positive self-esteem). Taken altogether, these signal to the child that they are valued for what they say, do, and think - and that their uniqueness matters. It's not what they do – it is what they are that is of value.

Why then are not all children of unhealthy narcissists, unhealthy narcissists themselves? Fact is many children will go another developmental route, called co-dependency. The co-dependent child learns to please the unhealthy narcissistic parent foregoing their own internal needs. The parent gives approval instead of love to the co-dependent child and thus co-dependent's learn to be pleasers in order to get gratification. They also learn to read the cues of the unhealthy parent thus promoting hypervigilance.

The co-dependent child is the unseen child. They are simply extensions of the N-parent. They are not acknowledged as their own independent person. What the co-dependent person lacks is empathic expression from the unhealthy parent. This vital empathic response also extends to a lack of respect and understanding, plus overall tolerance for the developing child.

Take look at the unhealthy narcissist in your life.

- Do they see you for who you really are?
- Are they understanding and have empathy?
- Do they tolerate and respect your feelings?

Empathy is not just saying you understand, but demonstrating it through positive physical behavior and gesturing. One of my new mantras about unhealthy narcissists is: *Believe what they do and not what they say*. It should also be noted and emphasized that the unhealthy narcissist cannot delay gratification.

They choose to gratify their own needs ahead of everyone else and also to the exclusion of others needs. As the late Swiss psychoanalyst Alice Miller points out in her groundbreaking book, Drama of the Gifted Child, pg. 21, they are unable to be "honest and available, helpful and loving, feeling, transparent, or clear without unintelligible contradictions."

It is on the subject of contradictions and contrariness that my book begins.

CHAPTER 1

In Through the Out Door

Identifying the Unhealthy Narcissist and their Qualities

One of my favorite Led Zeppelin albums is, "In Through the Out Door". It has always reminded me of Alice in Wonderland and the upside down turned around world she found herself in after falling down the rabbit hole. That is what it is like when you fall down the rabbit hole of the world of an unhealthy narcissist. It is fascinating at first, wondrous one might say, and then things begin to get all fouled up.

"I see you're admiring my little box," the Knight said in a friendly tone. "It's my own invention - to keep clothes and sandwiches in. You see I carry it upside down, so that the rain can't get in." from Alice in Wonderland, by Lewis Carroll.

Alice's adventures in wonderland are a fairytale, but encounters with unhealthy narcissists, especially extreme narcissists (also called malignant narcissists), are the furthest thing from a fairytale. It is a disturbing reality they live in and one which you must avoid. If you get sucked into their void they can ruin your life. The problem is, they look like everyone else and most are quite sane. Let's take a look at some of their hallmark traits and control tactics to help separate out the unhealthy narcissist from the rest of us. Once you can identify and understand some of their traits, common control tactics, and the roots of their behavior you will get a better idea of where and how you fit into the unhealthy narcissist's dynamic.

Contrariness

As logical as many unhealthy narcissists seem, one of the hallmark behaviors of an unhealthy narcissist (who, for convenience, I will also refer to as an N-person), is contrariness. They will say up is down, black is white, this is that, etc. They will contradict, change their minds, change plans, show up late, say you did not say something when you know you did, and conveniently forget things they have said or did. This type of behavior is enough to make any person doubt their own actions, if not their own minds.

Their penchant towards contrariness results in subterfuge. Subterfuge (creating doubt in the other person), is an effective control tactic that the N-person uses to keep others off balance while retaining control over them. One of the key aspects to understanding any N-person is their need to control what I call their 'N-space'. Everything within the N-space is viewed as an extension of the N-person, thus to maintain their sense of control that fuels their sense of security and enables their false self to function, they use various tactics to control everything within their N-space – including you.

Props and Scenery

The N-space can be anywhere: the home, the office, the car, your home or your car, or any other space where the N-person projects their dominance. It's all just props and scenery to them. Dominance is their thing. It's what they do – dominate. Through dominance the N-person sets the agenda for any given situation. They show up late for a meeting and accordingly all eyes are on them. They are greeted and then ask for a refreshment, and then, and only then can the meeting continue. Take note when you observe the habitual late arriving person. Habitual lateness is a sign of disrespect for others, but for the N-person it is a statement that your time means nothing and more importantly - they are setting the agenda.

No matter the venue, people are treated as objects by the N-person. They live by an unconscious script that is part and parcel of their personality. Thus, if you misbehave, meaning, not meet their expectations, they will use a control tactic to bring you back into compliance. You must act a certain way, be a certain way and not deviate. Never mind that this treatment is blatant disregard for your very person, or for the autonomy and self-determination that everyone is entitled to – the N-person's viewpoint and psychological orientation is that they are the only one entitled to anything and everything; they run the show; it's their show. They make the rules and set the agenda and everyone is expected to comply.

The term, God-complex, was used for a long time to describe people with unhealthy narcissism. The God-complex goes something like this: They know - you don't. They are superior - you are not. They are entitled - you are not. And do not challenge them. Everything and everyone exists to serve the N-person. Sounds very much like a King, or a young child. The fact is, they <u>are</u> a young child. They are not just emotionally lacking, they are adults who are grossly immature as they did not successfully transition the stage of individuation in their childhood. It is important to understand this point: Because of their maladapted personality, their unhealthy narcissism is fixed -- it <u>is</u> their perpetual state. Many experts posit that the unhealthy narcissist is stuck at a pre-separation infantile stage where they are locked into the parental dependence phase of development of their personality.

Parental Dependence

We can understand the N-personality better by understanding parental dependence. As young children, humans are dependent upon parents for everything – food, love, nurturing, etc. Our entire environment is provided by the parental figure. Somewhere around 15-18 months we begin to separate from our parents. We walk, we explore, we venture further and further away from mother or father. The healthy parent will encourage our explorations and our curiosity and they will comfort us when we feel a little fear at our going too far and also encourage us to go further. But, when the parent does not allow exploration, or objects to satisfying our innate curiosity, and then scolds us for not behaving as they wish, they are interfering with the natural course of child development - with our becoming independent. The result is the parental figure stifles the child's natural curiosity to explore their world and expand their range of experiences which helps promote personality development. The result is the N-parent retains the child's dependency on them which in turn feeds their own controlling narcissism. Read carefully: the N-child becomes a dependent personality by being denied the natural course of separation from their unhealthy narcissistic parent.

Even though they project superiority and are described as condescending, aloof and arrogant, experts say they also feel fragile, empty and worthless inside. I think of them as perpetually lost in a world of grownups where they are trying to function but with a set of personality skills that do not match the test. Thus, the unhealthy narcissist depends on others to provide for them and do for them - and they expect it to be so. And though the N-person may be very successful financially, they are infantile in their emotional behavior for the rest of their life. And it is their demanding, infantile and exacting behavior that often turns into abuse towards others.

"Personality Assessment: to define and to understand the diversity of human traits, the many ways people have of thinking and perceiving and learning and emoting. Such nonmaterial human dimensions, types, and attributes are constructs—in this case, in-

ferences drawn from observed behavior. Widely stud-ied personality constructs include anxiety, hostility, emotionality, motivations and introversion-extroversion."

Source: Encyclopedia Britannica, Personality Assessment

"In personal construct theory, we find that humans develop internal models of reality, called constructs in order to understand and explain the world around them. Constructs are often defined by words, but can also be non-verbal and hard to explain. When constructs are challenged or incomplete the result is emotional states such as anxiety, confusion, anger and fear."

Source: Personal Construct Theory, Changing-Minds.org

So, we come to find that in early childhood the developing dependent self cannot separate and break free from the parental figure, that their dependency and the pattern of having someone (the parent, care-taker, or archetypal figure), satisfy all their essential needs is now the premise from which a false-self be-comes permanently established. The die is cast and the N-child can no longer experience an evolving, in-dependent, core self. The result is the child retains a grandiose false-self. Thus, the grandiose false-self be-gets arrested emotional development and unhealthy narcissistic personality problems. It is a fractured per-sonality that emerges, one which can function in the world, but has a flawed worldview, with an overdeveloped set of expectations, and an underdeveloped set of emotions.

This false-personality construct of overdeveloped expectations sets up the N-person for future frustration when reality does not match up to their N-fantasies; plus, their underdeveloped emotions put them at a distinct disadvantage to cope with such frustrations. This paradigm sets the stage for narcissistic rage.

Otherness

It is not difficult to understand that while it is perfectly fine to cater to an infant or very young child, it is not ok to cater to an older child, teenager, or adult. As we develop, we all must learn to set boundaries, respect others, and assume more and more responsibility for ourselves - for our own lives. We are no longer entitled to cry to be fed or changed, or call out to be picked up and coddled. We must learn to interact with others – we must learn *otherness*. And this inability for unhealthy narcissists to acknowledge otherness it seems is the root of all their relationship problems. Warning: when you hook up with an N-person, your otherness is in for a world of trouble, meaning – check your otherness at the door. They do not see you. You are part of the N-space.

Unhealthy narcissists will claim to love their children, their spouse or their sibling, but too often they say things like, "Your opinions don't matter." or,

" No one is interested in your opinions or what you have to say." or, "You don't know that!" or, "How do you know that?" Those kinds of contrary and accusatory statements are a denial of otherness and thus a denial of your very existence. What the N-person is actually saying is they are unable to acknowledge that what you say means anything to them, or matters to them, and therefore no one cares. They cannot lend validity to what others say as they do not recognize otherness. They are unable to see beyond their own selves and see you for who you are – you, a living, and breathing, multi-dimensional human being! Thus, rather than acknowledging others thoughts and feelings, they judge. BTW: they will say these things often in the form of a proclamation or pronouncement - another tip off that you may be dealing with an N-person.

Many unhealthy narcissists are intelligent people who engage in high functioning professions where collaboration matters, but their collaborative ability is narrow in scope in that they will acknowledge only what they can use to further themselves. And too often they will take credit for all the work done.

What else is at work in the N-personality when they make claims they care about a person, yet make negative statements? Answer: Envy.

Envy

Envy is one of the hallmark traits of an unhealthy narcissist. The N-person envies others who have skills, status, abilities or qualities that they themselves do not possess. Let's deconstruct this.

The N-person cannot self-reflect – as in, oh I did a bad thing, or I hurt someone, or I was insensitive – shame on me. Why is it that they cannot self-reflect? Answer: Because the true self is *sublimated*. It is theorized that a person cannot reflect back on something that is not developed in their psyche. What we find instead, is a false-self, the grandiose-self, a psychological construct with only the basic personality traits and primitive emotions holding it together. The N-person is unable to think, 'oh this person is different than me and possesses different talents, skills, opinions, etc. and how great is that?' To compare themselves to others means to be vulnerable to attacks they cannot handle, so we find the N-person fiercely guarding their false-self. They are unable to recognize otherness and differences, thus, rather than admiring others, they do the opposite - they envy. And they not only envy others their talents and skills, they envy the person, their very being, their autonomy, the fact that they are a grown up with grown up feelings and qualities (something they will never truly experience).

Sublimate: to modify the natural expression of (a primitive, instinctual impulse) in a socially acceptable manner.

An N-person's envy is a projection of their own deep-seated unconscious feelings of inadequacies. Thus, they envy and they compete with others - and this drives their constant need to dominate others.

It is important to understand that the envy of an un-healthy narcissist can often turn to rage (called narcissistic rage), as they are frustrated at their own inability to accept that others are smarter, more skilled, or superior to them in terms of achievement or expertise. Thus, their deep seated deficiencies drive the N-person to become controlling and this is where unhealthy narcissism can develop into abusive behavior.

Trait: a distinguishing quality; an inherited characteristic.

Envy leads many narcissists to role-playing. They like dress-up. They are by their very nature, performers. They mirror what they admire, just like little kids. I was once told by one after I said I too liked Bob Dylan (as they claimed they were a big fan), "you don't understand, I want to be Bob Dylan." It was said in dead earnest. That was one of those moments where I recognized that the person had serious self-image problems.

Tied to their envy, the N-person also has problems with being impulsive, some would say reckless in their behavior. Let's not cut these people any slack: they cannot control their impulsivity because they cannot self reflect. They cannot see the consequences of their own actions. Think of them as very young children. When a youngster does these things we think how cute or clever, they are just playing and they will grow out of it and grow up – meaning they will mature. But when a grown adult acts impulsively, it can be not only disruptive, but destructive – to themselves and others. Many unhealthy narcissists are not only impulsive, but compulsive, like compulsive shoppers, gamblers, workaholics, addicts, etc; and, it is all too common for the N-person to also be a habitual abuser.

Mirroring

This is where the pathology of unhealthy narcissism starts to get a little scary. As noted, unhealthy narcissists are people who live their life by a script. They live out patterns of behavior over and over again. Like most people, as they develop and grow up they come to realize what works for them, and what does not work. And like all humans the N-person needs to interact with other people, regardless of the fact that they treat others as objects. But the N-person needs others for a very different reason: they need other people to work through their internal script.

The N-Pattern Behavior Script: Approach-Assess-Accept-Inflate-Deflate/Devalue

If there is one thing I finally understood from all my research is that there is a definite pattern in the way unhealthy narcissists associate with others. They behave in specific ways to bring people into their lives. Learn this and you will be far along in recognizing the signs of how they suck you into their vortex of illusion. So if this starts happening to you again, you can avoid the ultimate unpleasant and painful outcome – deflation and devaluation.

How It Works

The N-person seeks out people who will help them through their mental script. It starts like this, they approach someone (they are masters at assessing quickly whether a person can be useful to them), if assessed as someone they can use, or will be useful, they will then begin something called the mirroring phase. It's a flawless performance. It's all automatic for these people.

Think back on your encounter with an unhealthy narcissist. In the earliest phase of your "relationship" everything was peachy. You and the N-person got on splendidly, almost too good to be true. You were *simpatico*; maybe you even thought you were soul-mates. What is happening at this stage is they are mirroring your qualities. It is automatic, they cannot help it and for your part, you enjoy the attention and interaction - why not? You think, they are in sync with you, and it is a great feeling when someone really "gets you." Except the reality is what the N-person is actually doing is mirroring you and your best qualities. Understand: they mirror what they envy. What you see in them is the unhealthy narcissist reflecting your good qualities back to you. Wow! Let's reread that one. No wonder you feel like they get you, they are you, but just for a brief span of time. They cannot maintain the mirroring for long. So, you feed back to them good feelings and energy and thus begins a kind of dance, a back and forth of energies, an N- courtship where you think you are in a super relationship, a soul mate friendship, or fated partnership.

(Important to note: Mirroring, - yes; reciprocating, – no. Unhealthy narcissists cannot have reciprocal relationships. They experience something more on the order of an interpersonal dynamic, but devoid of mature reciprocal feelings. This will become more apparent as you read on.)

Add to the mirroring stage, the inflation stage: the compliments, the charm, the flattery and ego boosting. They put you up on a pedestal. It is mighty fine indeed, while it lasts. It is where many get hooked. The N-person can make you feel great! They pump you up, make you feel energized, and life is good. And then all of a sudden it all changes. Maybe it is a few months, maybe a few years, but it will change and it happens in a very distinct and very noticeable manner.

I have read many accounts of women who say the guy they were dating was perfect. (Just a note: there is no such thing as perfect, or a perfect match, and certainly not a perfect person; that kind of admiration is actually something called *idealization*).

"Idealization and devaluation: When an individual is unable to integrate difficult feelings, specific defenses are mobilized to overcome what the individual perceives as an unbearable situation. The defense that helps in this process is called splitting. Splitting is the tendency to view events or people as either all bad or all good. When viewing people as all good, the individual is said to be using the defense mechanism **idealization***: a mental mechanism in which the person*

13

*attributes exaggeratedly positive qualities to the self or others. When viewing people as all bad, the individual employs **devaluation**: attributing exaggeratedly negative qualities to the self or others."*

"In child development idealization and devaluation are quite normal. During the childhood development stage, individuals become capable of perceiving others as complex structures, containing both good and bad components. If the development stage is interrupted (by early childhood trauma, for example), these defense mechanisms may persist into adulthood. The term idealization first appeared in connection with Freud's definition of narcissism."

Source: Wikipedia, Idealization and devaluation

So, everything is wonderful when the N-person is idealizing their future mate. Then they get married and like a switch going on (or off) the dream guy turns into a changed person – think Jekyll & Hyde. The controlling starts, the slights, the intimidation, the insults, the diminishing, the abuse – the devaluation. What has happened?

The N-person lives by a script – remember? And after the initial approach, assess, accept and inflation phase, the deflation and devaluation phase begins. Why? Because the N-person is superior to all, even those they profess to love because they see them as objects; (you cannot love objects - you can admire them, treasure them, but not love them). The N-person therefore mimics love. They act out what they have

14

seen others do. So, as things progress they experience ever increasing anxiety as the other person is thinking they have a real, adult relationship going. They will even have sexual relations and appear to be fully engaged, but as with all healthy relationships there eventually is the next step – that of deep emotional intimacy. And this is where crisis occurs for the N-person. Intimacy is the one thing you cannot fake and it's the one thing they cannot do.

Reciprocation: To show, feel, or give in response or return.

The crisis for the N-person is deep intimacy requires trust and vulnerability. With an N-person they cannot emotionally reciprocate at this level because they simply do not know how – and this is because they are emotionally underdeveloped and more importantly, they see others as objects. Why on Earth (they reason), would they want to be on par with an object? Plus, we must understand that in all cases the object is inferior to the N-person and if they were to become equal to the object-other, this would diminish their false-self. And to feel vulnerable for the unhealthy narcissist is a frightening affair as they do not want to expose their false-self and be found out.

The key here is to understand the unhealthy narcissist unconsciously suppresses shame as they were not allowed to feel shame as a developing child (shame implies imperfection – oops, I did something wrong), thus, they will not submit themselves to the risky emotion of intimacy, an emotion that would overwhelm them and risk exposing their false-self. So, they turn this anxiety on its head and push away the object-other. The result: the other person, the source of their anxiety, must be devalued. The N-person simply will not tolerate others who challenge their superior false-self paradigm, thus they must, and are compelled to tear down anyone who challenges their paradigm. To aid in supporting their paradigm, they also have an over-developed Super-ego. The N-Super-ego helps to protect the false-self (reminder: the false-self is a maladapted fragmented personality). The N-Super-ego will support the false self's notion that the N-person is superior and they will stop at nothing to remind their spouse again and again that that is the way it is. The spouse, cannot be equal, they must be lesser than - always. In business, it is the same. They will not share successes and are very poor team players. They are fierce competitors taking down their co-workers like a lion takes down its prey.

For those of you who have been on the receiving end of this behavior you know this is no exaggeration. Many experts in this field of study say one thing about unhealthy narcissists: Get away and stay away (Chapter Three).

The sad and terrible truth is unhealthy narcissists leave a path of destruction in their wake. Before you know what has hit you they have already moved on to another kill, another drama. They thrive on drama. They thrive on the take-down. It is important to note, the very extreme ones are psychopaths, otherwise known as sociopaths.

Control Tactics

The control tactics used by the unhealthy narcissist have been identified by experts in the field. (See References) Lying is one of them. They are terrific liars – true masters of the half-lie/half-truth. They let the perverted truth roll off their tongue without compunction. While lying is viewed as immoral, for the N-person, who makes their own rules, it is an expedient way to get what they want. Children tell half-lies so as to not take responsibility for a wrong they have committed. The half-truth sounds so much like the truth that it is used interchangeably with the real truth. It is not a matter of morality, but one of convenience.

The N-child, as an adult, is never wrong and will find ways to offload shame onto others. They do not apologize for their errant behavior. In fact, they will turn situations around to make it appear someone else is to blame – oftentimes that's you. Again, they live their life by a script. You will not convince them of their culpability or error of their ways. Remember, they have had a whole lifetime of "practice" behaving and deceiving this way -- and years of being reinforced by others too blind to see what they are doing. Thus the terms, *slick as a whistle,* or *smooth operator* aptly applies.

It is also important to note that the N-person loves hyperbole. They will use flattery, compliments and hype to manipulate others to do things for them that they otherwise would not do for themselves. They butter people up. I was told by one N-person how amazing I was over and over again until after awhile I realized this was a term they used to get people to cooperate and do things for them. Believe you me; they know just what to say and how to say it. They are masters at mind games.

Hypervigilance

How do they do it? How do they get under peoples skin? How do they read people so well? Answer: N-persons are skilled observers. They are adept at getting to know peoples weaknesses and what buttons to push. This is called hypervigilance, or watchful observance. On the website *Help4trauma.org* I found this explanation:

"For many, "hypervigilance" is a natural response following trauma, whereby your mind and body instinctively remain alert to any additional potential threats, real or imagined, to your wellbeing. Hypervigilance can be an outcome of the anxiety experienced as part of Acute Stress Disorder or Post Traumatic Stress Disorder. Feelings of hypervigilance can come and go at different times, often trigged by certain people or situations. "

"During a time of heightened hypervigilance, many survivors experience strong bursts of nervous energy- a drive to keep "doing something." Often this energy is subconsciously aimed at managing the anguish, pain, and anger resulting from their violent experience. Symptoms of hypervigilance can include

sleeplessness, anxiety, panic attacks, and obsessive or obsessive-compulsive behavior. It is important to recognize hypervigilance and to try to channel that energy into constructive activities, and to find a way to rest and relax."

What we come to understand is unhealthy narcissists had abusive childhoods. The abuse was physical, emotional, psychological or sexual or a combination thereof. They might have been neglected or severely punished, or the opposite: glorified and put on a pedestal. Children of alcoholics often suffer from this syndrome. I myself came from a family of an alcoholic, overbearing father and a perfectionist, passive-aggressive mother. Both, I believe, suffered from unhealthy narcissism. Both were verbal and emotional abusers; my father was physically abusive. To this very day I get very anxious before seeing my elderly parent, even though I know this person can no longer hurt me, I steel myself for another offhanded remark, criticism, or verbal insult.

In the world of the abused child you find they are often hypervigilant – meaning, on guard to make sure no one will hurt them. They have learned that it is beneficial to be on the alert for another episode of abuse and thus are scouting their environment for any potential threat. This is mostly an unconscious effort, but I know for myself, I become very anxious before seeing my parents and am very dialed-in to my parents behavior in their presence.

Hypervigilant children and adults are excellent at anticipating the rise of chaotic behavior enabling them to step in and quell the anxiety as quickly as possible. It is an effective strategy, but it is also an exhausting way to live. And while it may sound like I am an unhealthy narcissist, I am the opposite; I am the CD, or co-dependent personality. The CD is the people pleaser, the fixer, the make-nice person. They were often the ignored or bullied child. They were the ones who tried to diffuse the toxic buildup in the family: make daddy laugh, please the upset or demanding parent. There are many things in common between the two personality types, like what type of family they came from, and each (the unhealthy narcissist and the co-dependent), have their own set of control tactics. For CDs it is over pleasing, over accommodation and over compliance. Another example of how I knew I was dealing with an unhealthy narcissist (the one who inspired this book), is I asked one day, "Do I make you feel calm?" They answered in a quiet, childlike tone, "Yes." The problem here is that in the N/CD dynamic the CD finds themselves emotionally drained in being an emotional conduit for the N-person. I often felt quite drained after visiting with this person.

Thankfully people with co-dependent personalities can change and improve. Because they are sensitive and empathic persons they can learn to change through self-reflection, and self-reflection means a person can analyze their behavior and change it. From what I have read the overall consensus is because the N-person lacks empathy and cannot self-reflect, they will not and cannot change, nor improve - and most have no motivation to do so. Why change when you think you are oh-so perfect and oh-so wonderful and vastly superior to others?

So, how do we – the damaged, but healthy ones and CDs - change and improve? In my forward I stated the first thing we must do is forgive. As difficult as this is, we must forgive ourselves and forgive others who have hurt us. That is not to say we should forget, nor protect ourselves from further abuse. I am of the firm belief that we must remember and learn from our past so we can be free from it. Then and only then can we reshape our lives.

CHAPTER 2

Pattern Behavior

Digging a little deeper: Why do they do those things?

People that are on occasion rude, crude and obnoxious are not always unhealthy narcissists. They may be just annoying. But the person who has a pervasive and repetitious pattern of being rude, crude and obnoxious may be displaying underlying traits of unhealthy narcissism.

Rudeness is related to arrogance. Crudeness is related to immaturity. Being obnoxious is related to attention getting. These are but a few of the behavior traits of an unhealthy narcissist. Humor can be used as weapon to diminish others:

(i) Hostile humor (hurting someone to laugh), (ii) superiority humor (laughing at someone's short comings), (iii) or authority-rebellion humor (laughing at unfunny, smutty jokes).

As many other books have done, I will lay out the behavior patterns as described by the DSM-IV, Diagnostic and Statistical Manual of Mental Disorders, the diagnostic classification system used in the United States. I will also provide some additional background as to how unhealthy narcissism develops that lends to this type behavior.

A pervasive pattern of grandiosity (in fantasy or behavior), the need for admiration, and lack of empathy - beginning by early adulthood and present in a variety of contexts, as indicated by five (or more) of the following:

(1) has a grandiose sense of self-importance (e.g., exaggerates achievements and talents, expects to be recognized as superior without commensurate achievements)

(2) is preoccupied with fantasies of unlimited success, power, brilliance, beauty, or ideal love

(3) believes that he or she is "special" and unique and can only be understood by, or should associate with, other special or high-status people (or institutions)

(4) requires excessive admiration

(5) has a sense of entitlement, i.e., unreasonable expectations of especially favorable treatment or automatic compliance with his or her expectations

(6) is interpersonally exploitative, i.e., takes advantage of others to achieve his or her own ends

(7) lacks empathy: is unwilling to recognize or identify with the feelings and needs of others

(8) is often envious of others or believes that others are envious of him or her

(9) shows arrogant, haughty behaviors or attitudes

You might want to stop right here and study those behaviors for awhile, maybe even a few days.

The first time I came across this list I was bowled over. However, most of what I read clicked into place for I knew not only one person, but several people I have known, including my family members, who were indeed unhealthy narcissists. Although it was not a good day for me, it was a revelation and relief as I wrote in my journal, "it has a name".

After many years of dealing with a known quantity - an alcoholic father and a passive-aggressive mother, I thought I had come to end of the road of understanding what had gone on in my dysfunctional family: alcoholism and passive-aggression. But with new information in hand, what I came to understand was underlying those dysfunctions was something else, something much more disturbing: unhealthy narcissism. My parents are elderly now and cannot defend themselves, so I will not go into the personal dynamics of my family, nor will I reveal any behaviors of persons close to me -- that would not be the fair, nor honorable thing to do. I will try however to explain why unhealthy narcissists do the things they do.

First, I want to reiterate what has been said: unhealthy narcissism displays itself through a pervasive pattern of behavior primarily egotistical in nature with an exaggerated sense of self-importance.

Here is a list of words that describe common behaviors and traits:

- Arrogant
- Acts Entitled

- Braggart
- Bully
- Coercive
- Conceited
- Contrary
- Charming
- Critical
- Demanding
- Emotionally Remote
- Guileless
- Haughty
- Judgmental
- Lacks Empathy
- Manipulative
- Non-reciprocating
- Over confident
- Recalcitrant

And these:

- Black and white thinking is prevalent
- Body language that imparts an air of superiority
- Charming to a fault - but not intimate
- Compliments or gushes; or the opposite, insults or ignores
- Demands to do everything their way
- Demands undivided attention
- Demanding in being treated preferentially
- Emotionally remote and territorial, i.e. owns the space
- Seeks and expects attention

- Will be polite and do what is socially expedient; and conversely will issue barbs and slights
- Will ingratiate themselves, name drop; try to belong yet remain aloof and remote

Important: Unhealthy narcissism manifests itself on a sliding scale from mild unhealthy narcissism to full blown NPD, narcissistic personality disorder, to the most extreme, the psychopath or sociopath.

Not One Thing

Remember, it is not one thing, or a few things. If it is only a few of the above traits mentioned, you are likely dealing with a control freak. To be sure, control freaks (do it my way), can do a great deal of psychological and emotional damage to others and their behavior should not be excused nor underestimated, but in fact scrutinized and avoided. Control freaks impinge on others boundaries and if allowed to control the, *who, what, where and when* of another's life will negatively impact the other person's self-confidence. Many a con man is a control freak and will fleece others who are unwitting victims in their nefarious dealings: think of recent Ponzi-schemes. The controller will charm, cajole, infer their own authority or expertise, and otherwise behave in ways to persuade others to forgo their own good judgment. When you are making a decision against your own good judgment that should be a red flag.

Theories

I came to my own conclusion on how unhealthy narcissism develops based on studying many experts in the field, but in particular, Heinz Kohut. Kohut was an Austrian-born psychoanalyst who founded the school of thought called, Self Psychology. He developed his ideas around what he called the tripartite (three-part) self.

"According to Kohut, this three-part self can only develop when the needs of one's "self states," including one's sense of worth and well-being, are met. Kohut was thus the first dynamic theorist to emphasize the importance of relationships."

Source: Wikipedia, Heinz Kohut

Also, according to Kohut's biographer Charles Strozier, Kohut's book, *The Analysis of the Self: A Systematic Analysis of the Treatment of the Narcissistic Personality Disorders* "had a significant impact on the field by extending Freud's theory of narcissism and introducing what Kohut called the 'self-object transferences' of mirroring and idealization." In other words, children need to idealize and emotionally "sink into" the competence of empathic, caregiving others; this allows them to thereby learn the self-soothing and other skills that are necessary for a healthy sense of self.

My ongoing research and reflection of my own experience has led me to believe (as Kohut and many others do), that we have a core self and when we are developing in our early years we develop our personality in a way to cope with our world. If we are nurtured properly, loved in healthy ways, validated in balanced ways, and given boundaries we will develop a healthy "true self" – meaning we will adapt in a healthy way. If we lack those conditions we will develop a "false-self" based on our early grandiose self and our personality will be maladapted. Humans absolutely must develop their personality as a means to cope and deal with the outside world - and it will adapt accordingly. The idea behind the unhealthy narcissist is they are maladapted. The N-person's personality has adapted in such a way so as to compensate for the lack of healthy conditions (nurturing, guidance, support, continuity and love) during their early development.

"Kohut believed that children begin life with 'fantasies about a grandiose self and ideal parents'. 'If normal development occurs, the grandiose self illusion is transformed into healthy self-esteem and the ideal parents illusion becomes a 'basis for our strongest values'. (Emundson, 2001)"

"If something goes wrong in childrearing, if the parenting process is badly flawed, the grandiose self remains unchanged at its core so that the person develops a Narcissistic Personality Disorder. This disorder is revealed in depressiveness, irritability, edginess, and an anger proneness. A person with this disorder is constantly in need of affirmation from outside because he believes that he is a superstar, a hero

who ought to be treated as such. However, life experi-
ence does not fit in with this delusion and so he feels
rage either towards himself or towards the world.'
(Edmundson, 2001)"

The person with a healthy personality has a cohesive sense of self. Everything is there: empathy, compassion, conscience, discernment, depth of emotion, good boundaries, mutual respect, sensitivity, etc. One of the most important traits however, is empathy. Empathy is something mirrored to us by healthy parents and/or caregivers. Parental empathy allows children to learn to become aware of others and develop a sense of "otherness". Empathy is essential to developing and recognizing boundaries and most importantly, to developing our moral center. It could be we learned from our grandparents, or aunts or cousins, or even an attentive neighbor. So, if the parent was an N-parent, the child might have other input during their developmental years and therefore opportunity to develop empathy. Being around other adult figures and siblings is important in learning good boundaries. Boundaries help us develop mutual respect. Empathy plays a role in developing our moral center. A moral center is what helps us to control our impulses so we do not hurt others or exploit others. Empathy is also tied to helping us to live ethical lives, one where we honor fair play and not cheat others. I believe it also is what propels us to rise above ourselves and to do good for our communities and our greater world.

Kohut's theories are helpful in understanding the importance of empathy. He focused on empathic relationships and what he called, *Dynamic Object Relations theory.*

"The theory describes the process of developing a mind as one grows in relation to others in the environment. The "objects" of the theory are both real others in one's world, and one's internalized images of others. Object relationships are initially formed during early interactions with primary care givers. These early patterns can be altered with experience, but often continue to exert a strong influence throughout life."

Source: Wikipedia, Heinz Kohut

The Center of the World

Early childhood development is the key to understanding unhealthy narcissism. Through no fault of the child, we find that one, or both parents, likely suffered from unhealthy narcissism. In the case of a child who develops unhealthy narcissism, the needs of the unhealthy narcissistic parents (mother, father, or both), came first. Their inability to properly nurture their child through the important early stages of personality development impacts the child's ability to complete healthy separation from the parental figure thereby relegating the child to remain a dependent personality with a maladapted set of narcissistic traits.

A young child, who is inhibited from emerging from the phase of the hermetic world of feeling extraordinary and omnipotent, will continue to live as though they are the center of the world. They remain in the perfect world of the dependent infant. Children who do not get past this stage then have difficulty in learning recognition of *otherness*. Others then, simply take on the role of providers - they are part of the N-environment, as mentioned in Chapter One: props and scenery, meaning they are part of the N-person's background.

This is problematic for the N-child for if they cannot empathize with others they will have problems with personal boundaries and interpersonal relationships. This unfortunate child will experience a lifetime of frustration, high anxiety and persistent pathological problems.

It should be noted that while it is not my intent to delve into all the psychology behind unhealthy narcissism, I do want to empower the reader with enough information to help them identify what it is, how it manifests itself, and how to manage their life and/or move away from these people into a healthier way of being.

The bottom line is the N-person is grossly immature. They are the little tyrant. They are the, *I am never wrong person, I want it now person* and *Do it my way* person. Their unhealthy narcissism can be masked in a variety of ways. Many are very intelligent and very successful, but invariably they have poor interpersonal track records. That's because they use others, manipulate others, exploit others and generally are poor partners. Behaviors the N-person would never tolerate, they perpetrate upon others on a regular basis. While they have tight boundaries, they trample all over other people's boundaries. What is important to understand is the N-person needs an ever present source of attention to support their fragile false-self and will get it through exhibiting charm, confidence, high energy, and a larger than life persona. All of these traits act in concert with control tactics to establish their dominance.

Dominance and Attention

While most of us desire social connectedness, the unhealthy narcissist desires social dominance. They must be the King or Queen of the hill, alone in their loftiness (or, they are part of an N-group who feel and claim superiority). Remember they feel they are the center of the world. Their desire stems from their uber-feelings of entitlement. Think of Nietzsche's term *übermensch* to describe the higher state to which he felt man might aspire. Then think, Nazis. Same dynamic – and similar destructive results: I am better than you, in fact, you are nothing. If you are nothing it makes it so much easier to hurt you and even - destroy you.

Let's be real: Nazi's – who were nothing more than extreme bullies - gassed and burned millions of people who they considered inferior: Jews, homosexuals, artists, intellectuals, the old, infirmed, mentally handicapped, Poles and Russians and others they considered "impure" or "inferior". Their reasoning was they were on a fated mission of world domination through global conquest. Combined with the fascistic Empire of Japan and Mussolini's Italy, their pathology was pure collective narcissism with extreme grandiosity at the center. Here is the cost of their extremist behavior:

- Estimated military deaths from all campaigns in WWII: 22 to 25 million
- Estimated civilian deaths: 40 to 52 million people

For the Nazi's and other extreme unhealthy narcissists, people are things, objects to control, existing only for their usefulness and pleasure – remember, part of the environment. Think toys for tots in a very perverse way. The Nazi's had Jews do various useful and distasteful chores in the labor camps – like dispose of the bodies of other executed Jews, extract gold teeth and sort through the shoes and belongings of those who were interned who would later be murdered; and an even more twisted event - they had prisoners play classic music for the Nazi concentration camp officers. These same prisoners lived in terrible squalor surrounded by the stench of death everyday and were in a constant state of fear, yet expected to entertain their captors!

Once we digest these horrific facts, that people are things to the extreme unhealthy narcissist, we can arrive at the understanding of why having an extreme unhealthy narcissist in your life is not a good thing. You do not know the depths of their dysfunction. Loving one is bad, marrying one worse, and working for one a nightmare. In fact, when you are in any "relationship" with an extreme unhealthy narcissist, you are actually working for them, serving them, and doing their bidding. To what end you do not know and should not presume to know.

Deadly Charm

One of the most powerful forces of the unhealthy narcissist is their charm. I have experienced it first hand. It can be overpowering. I thought I had met my soul mate, twice in my life, but both persons turned out to be exploitive and highly insensitive. I found when in their presence I was off my game, and felt seduced into a near magical state of mind. This is not an unusual phenomenon for those exposed to N-charm - but it is also not reality. It taps into our own fantasies of a perfect mate, perfect love, soul mate, etc. and this makes us very vulnerable to manipulation. N-charm is used to reel people into the N-person's web. Why does the N-person charm us? They need attention and lots of it. In fact, they need an ongoing stream of attention, thus they will turn on the charm and get people to mirror back to them and thus begins the mirroring cycle that can send many people off the cliff into N-fantasyland.

"Serial killer Ted Bundy was described as a charming, articulate and intelligent man. Those were the traits that might have allowed him to get close to his victims. Bundy raped and / or murdered scores of women, strangling and mutilating his victims. Bundy often wore his arm in a sling or in a fake cast or his leg in a fake cast. He would ask his victims to help

him carry things to his car or help load or unload things from his car. Once the victims got in his car or were leaning into his car he would strike them over the head with a crowbar or pipe, after hitting his victims he would handcuff them to immobilize them."

Source: National Museum of Crime & Punishment

The N-person, in order to feel secure, must control and dominate his/her environment and everything and everyone in it. It is a constant. Their behavior springs from a very real need to perpetuate their false-self. As mentioned, the false-self is what developed in place of their true self in their early formative years. Well, if that isn't enough, research shows they have an over-the-top super ego to boot. I touched on this before. Let's take a closer look.

The super-ego for most of us governs our behavior, particularly our morality, our choices and our conscience. It helps keep us from exploiting and hurting others, or ourselves. The N-person's super-ego has developed in such a way that it exacts harsh judgment and is punishing, not only to others who threaten, or who they perceive as being threatening to their false-self, but also to their own false-self as well! The N-super-ego is what trips up the N-person from having any real success in life with others for they often unconsciously feel undeserving of love from others who get too close. Closeness poses a threat when one cannot reciprocate. When interacting with an N-person it is an unrealistic expectation.

So as we see, round and round it goes. But the reference here to the wheel of fortune is about the N-cycle that repeats itself over and over again. So, let's put the pieces together to better understand the repetitious patterning that is part and parcel of any unhealthy narcissist's life.

The Effective Use of Charm during the Approach-Assess-Accept phases

You meet a great person and they seem charming and full of life and energy and confidence. If this person is an N-person you are entering into the first stage in a cycle they repeat over and over. They are approaching someone that they are attracted to who may yield some usefulness. The charm is a feel-good optimistic ploy – a psychological control tactic. While you're feeling good all over, they are assessing you, sizing you up. They do it quickly and deftly. They are checking out your vulnerabilities, for what the N-person really is, is a predator. They are hunting for prey, hunting for others to exploit. As mentioned in the excellent book, *Stalking the Soul by Marie-France Hirogoyen*, unhealthy narcissists on the more extreme end are soul killers, and if psychopathic they are real killers.

To reiterate, the N-person wants and needs to dominate. They need people who will be subservient.

If you make it through this phase, they will accept you. You will know it. They will ratchet up the charm, the attention, the compliments, etc. This is called the inflation stage. They pump you up. They want to see you again - soon. You are now part of them, part of their world, a new thing, a new toy - a possession.

Subterfuge

No matter how long it lasts, eventually the N-person will devalue you. It is predictable and it is pure subterfuge. The definition of subterfuge is, "something intended to misrepresent the true nature of an activity". Ah! There it is - the definition of the modus operandi of an unhealthy narcissist. Remember it.

The take-down can be any number of things: insults, mind games, abuse at any level, lies, counter-lies, half-truths, deception, misleading statements, theft, bullying, neglect, and so on. It is a long laundry list. The goal is to diminish your self-esteem. They will want everything their way and you will have a dwindling say in what goes on. Your opinion and your self-defense are meaningless to the N-person.

If you have any sense of self (and self-preservation), you must take control of your life and leave. You may think it is love - and on your part, it may be, but for the N-person, there is no love as they cannot love as they cannot recognize otherness. They cannot experience vulnerability, or empathy, or recip-rocation. They depend on you for attention and adora-tion, that's it -- but it is not love.

Just a note: we love them, and for some after reading how the N-person was not loved or was mistreated as a child will say, I feel sorry for them, and will stay with them. I understand. BUT, and it is a big but, depending on the severity of the level of the unhealthy narcissism of the person you are involved with, these people will empty your bank account, they will exact all types of abuse, they do not respect you, they have no empathy for you. Ask yourself, what would happen to me if I got really sick? Is the N-person really capable of doing the right thing? And not just the right thing, can they care for you, can you trust them, can they be compassionate, sensitive and loving?

CHAPTER 3

It Takes Two

No matter what I do, they are never pleased.

Cliché? or perhaps an indicator of a dysfunctional relationship. As noted in Chapter Two, the N-person, or unhealthy narcissist, needs others to work through their life script. But they do have their preference of who they like doing it with - one being the CD, or co-dependent person. Why?

The CD, or co-dependent person, was also raised by a parental figure with unhealthy narcissism, but instead of becoming an N-person they went in another direction. Instead of being self-centered, they become other oriented. Where the N-person could give a hoot about others suffering, the CD wants to heal the world. They are very empathic, compassionate, conscientious, and exhibit a strong desire to fix, please and serve others. For the N-person they are a catch and highly desirable - but it is an ill-fated match, particularly for the CD. The N-person will suck the CD dry; they will take them for all they are worth. The CD will keep giving and giving and the N-person will keep taking and taking.

Why is it that no matter what you do for an unhealthy narcissist it never satiates them?

Because for the N-person the goal is not satisfaction or reciprocal appreciation – it is domination: they want to be always one up and others one down. They need providers to do for them, and if you are a CD, so much the better. The N-person must remain perpetually dominant in order to maintain their false-self and you cannot change that by giving, serving, or even loving them.... no matter how much or how well. Think, black hole.

The co-dependent who is geared towards serving and pleasing and fixing is often unfulfilled themselves. Why? Because they subordinate their own needs to others. And too often they are attracted to unhealthy narcissists to fulfill their own unconscious script: if I please you, you will give me approval, i.e. love. It is a symbiotic 'relationship' but one that is ultimately one-sided.

Where the CD is nurturing and caretaking, the N-person takes advantage and exploits those efforts turning them into ones of serving and pleasing the N-person. Where the CD is empathic and generous, the N-person lacks empathy and will attack the CD for being seemingly weak. Where the CD is overly sensitive and has difficulty asserting themselves to get their needs met due to self-doubt, the N-person will exploit their self-doubts through verbal abuse thus further devaluing the CD and destabilizing their psyche. The N-person feels more and more superior and the CD feels weaker and weaker. It is the ultimate N-trap.

While it looks pretty bad for the CD, it is important to note that unlike unhealthy narcissists, CD behaviors can change – and for the better. Many experts agree that CDs can engage in self-reflection and are able to modify their behavior. It is a blessing for the CD who can and then chooses to self-reflect, for this leads to self-awareness which can then lead to positive behavioral changes thus strengthening the authentic core self.

Breaking the Pattern

As previously noted, I am CD, or co-dependent. I have tempered and modified my CD behavior with decades of self-reflection, meditation, practicing a form of spiritual devotion, (called Sadhana), plus reading many books on psychology, philosophy, and human behavior. I also practice mindfulness, meaning I am aware of my behavior so I can control my compulsive actions: fix, please, appease or acquiesce. It can be very hard for me at times to contain the urge to want to please others. "Can I", and "Would you like", are big parts of my vernacular. The key is to become aware of your over-pleasing behavior and rein it in. Practicing mindfulness will help you tremendously.

Mindfulness is calm awareness of oneself: your inner self, your feelings, your consciousness, your memories, your surroundings and overall state of mind. When we become in touch with ourselves we can start to address inner conflicts, explore resolutions, and begin to unwind the gnarled thinking that has plagued us and caused us to act unwisely and in unhealthful ways. The goal is well-being. Well-being is harmony of your mind-body-emotions.

Here is a first step. When around a person who means something to you, someone you care about, you may find yourself automatically relegated to the role of servant, pleaser, supporting role, etc. Stop! Become aware of this behavior – yours and theirs. You can interrupt this dance of dominance-compliance by excusing yourself, leaving the premises, or choosing to not engage with the N-person. Do not be overly concerned in how the other person will react. Do what you need to do to change the dynamic for your tendency towards over compliant behavior is damaging to your self-esteem.

When you are constantly pleasing others and not tending to your own goals and priorities you are behaving in an unhealthy way. What happens is you believe other people's goals and priorities are more important than your own. This pattern of behavior is a direct result of unhealthy parenting where the N-parent's needs came first. Additionally, over accommodation is a CD control tactic that many healthy people do not like. It is tantamount to smothering – a violation of other's boundaries. Practice good boundaries.

The co-dependent person must learn new behaviors including:

- It is ok to say no
- It is ok to choose your wants & needs over someone else's
- It is not ok to be subservient – to anyone
- It is healthy to respect others boundaries
- It is healthy for others to respect your boundaries
- It is ok to assert yourself
- It is ok to defend yourself
- It is not ok to just drop whatever you are doing to meet someone else's demands (key word here is demands).

Let's take a closer look on how to break the pattern. Using mindfulness, take notice of what circumstances, which situations, and with whom you exhibit excessive pleasing behavior. What are unhealthy pleasing behaviors? Over accommodation, over compliance, eager willingness to appease or fix, and also acquiesce. When you choose others interests over your own on a regular basis, that pattern of behavior is unhealthy. Persisting in doing this feeds into self-esteem problems and over time can be emotionally exhausting. It also can undermine efforts for personal success. You may think you are living a full life, but it is an unbalanced one and done at the expense of your own personal growth and well-being.

Think more along the lines of personal fulfillment versus a full life. In strategizing where you want to be in your life think about working towards changing self-defeating behaviors and achieving more balance in how you expend energy.

- Keep negative people out of your life
- Do not let others undermine your efforts
- Stay focused and positive about your self and your goals

Personal fulfillment is not so much about things as it is about a way of thinking and being. It is intangible versus tangible. The goal is inner serenity (at peace with one's self), and confidence.

One of the challenges is how do we achieve serenity in a hectic and fast paced and ever-changing society?

Through self-reflection we can find the answers. We start by asking the basic questions: What do I want and why do I want it? Consider these types of goals in shaping your path:

- Develop compassion without attachment
- Work with integrity
- Make a positive difference in the world
- Develop a balance between self-interest & common interest

A little tip on serving the common good. Being an altruistic person is a wonderful thing to be. It can also be a trap for the co-dependent person. There are plenty of stories about people who work themselves to death in the service of others for the better good. Take heed. Well-being is about balance and moderation and living a life of integrity.

"Help others, but when you do that, do not forget yourself." The Buddha

In pursuing your new goals you must first be free of any pattern behavior or inclination to control others (controlling through pleasing behaviors). Then, embrace a life of integrity. Choose self-respect over self-interest. For some who read this they will say, "I know that!" But in examining our behavior too often we are not walking the walk. In fact, what this process is really about is re-parenting our selves. If we had parents who could not, would not, did not provide healthy parenting, we can start over – right now.

In Chapter 6, Taking Action, I suggest these actions:

- Establish space and distance from unhealthy narcissists
- Take responsibility for your actions
- Recover and rebuild your self-esteem
- Set short term achievable goals
- Accept support from others
- Dump the myth – embrace reality

All of these things imply that you be methodic about pursuing your new life. Make a plan. Revise it. Try it out. If things are not quite the way you want them to be – revise your plan again. Try to be patient with your progress, yet tenacious about moving forward in a positive way. If you commit yourself to right action and right thinking your life will begin to improve.

Approval as Conditional Love

"Immature love says: 'I love you because I need you.' Mature love says: 'I need you because I love you." Erich Fromm, The Art of Loving

The love of an unhealthy narcissist is the prior: it is unhealthy love based on need. The *need* is the desire for unlimited attention to support the grandiose false-self. Let's return to the N-parent and CD dynamic. The N-parent instilled in the CD-child that pleasing behaviors were the only way in which to receive love for this is what they, the N-parent, needed – to be pleased. Pleasing the parent was then a condition for receiving love. In fact, there was no love, only approval, and most of the time even that was rarely given. Love in our tender early years from our parent should not be conditional. It should be warm, supportive, encouraging, affectionate, nurturing and generous.

Let's be clear here. The N-parent or N-caregiver cannot interact with others in a mature reciprocal loving way and thus issues approval to their children instead of giving them love. This is fundamental to understanding the dynamic that is in play. It always goes back to the N-person maintaining dominance due to their inability to recognize otherness. Thus, the authentic core self of their own children suffers emotional neglect and lack of unconditional love.

Unfortunately, in the eyes of the CD-child they learn approval is love. Thus, as a CD, we go through our lives seeking approval, when in reality what we need is love. They are not the same.

I love dogs and have had them all my life. When they do what I ask them to do, I say good dog and I give them approval. Oftentimes though, when I am with them I give them bear hugs just because. That's love – just because. They did not have to earn it, or do a trick, or serve me in some way. I love them for the wonderful creatures they are.

"To love means to commit oneself without guarantee, to give oneself completely in the hope that our love will produce love in the loved person." Erich Fromm, The Art of Loving

CHAPTER 4

Get Out and Stay Out

"I'm the decider, and I decide what's best"
– George W. Bush April 18, 2006

When George W. Bush uttered that line it was the nail in the coffin for me - I knew he was a control freak. After my research, I now believe he has an un-healthy narcissistic personality. Truth be told, it was just one of many off the wall utterances he made over the course of his troubled Presidency. Of course he was "the decider", he was the President of the United States, but the implication was he was superior in every sense of the word and implied everybody else should not question his decision making; therefore, the underlying message was one of demanding acqui-escence and subservience. In the context of what was happening, saying the embattled Pentagon chief, Don-ald Rumsfield was doing a "fine job" despite calls for his resignation from six retired military generals, President Bush was defending his false-self through an aggressive statement, thus dominating everybody who questioned his decisions. After observing many of his weird and inappropriate behaviors for nearly six years, I realized he was suffering from serious person-ality problems. Here is one more:

October 29, 2002 "If this were a dictatorship, it would be a heck of a lot easier, just so long as I'm the dictator,"

Another one of my favorite lines is when Michael Corleone, played by the actor Al Pacino in the movie The Godfather, Part III, says, "Just when I thought I was out, they pull me back in." I understood what he was talking about: being controlled.

Controller or decider, call them what you will, when we find ourselves in the position where we can no longer endure negative controlling people who surround us in our life, who put us down and manipulate us to their own ends, we must acknowledge and accept that there is a problem. We must find a way to get out of those situations (remember, these are not reciprocal relationships); we must extract ourselves from the unhealthy narcissist's grip. Coincidentally, like the Corleones in the Godfather series, many criminals are unhealthy narcissists. They have no conscience and no empathy. They make their own rules. They are ruthless and arrogant. They feel entitled to abuse, or steal, or even murder. Bottom line - they leave a path of destruction in their life.

What this chapter is about is getting out and staying out of N-relationships. Actually, that's a misnomer. We have established the fact in previous chapters that Ns cannot really engage in reciprocal adult relationships - they can have dynamic interaction with others, but not healthy, adult reciprocal relationships. Why is this?

It is well established by experts in this field that N-persons treat others like objects, view others as extensions of themselves, and thus, cannot have real, reciprocal relationships with others. I have read that unhealthy narcissists fail at nearly every "relationship". The more appropriate way to view their failures is the N-person often leaves the other person when the person has outlived their usefulness. And if the other person leaves the N-person, it is out of desperation to get out from under their abusive control.

While unhealthy narcissism runs the gamut, from minor control freaks to extreme sociopaths, all N-persons are manipulators, controllers, and engage in covert (obvious) and overt (subtle) abuse. The extreme ones are sexual and physical abusers; the very extreme ones are psychopaths and sociopaths. So, I agree with the experts – get out and stay out!

Here are some signs you are with a full-blown unhealthy narcissist. This is my litmus test:

- If you feel you are being treated like an object
- If you feel you are being treated like a servant
- If you find there is a total lack of intimacy - sex yes, intimacy no
- If you find that you are being told what to do and how to do it
- If you get pulled into arguments without cause
- If you find the N-person unloading on you (shame-dumping)
- If you find the N-person never apologizes for their bad behavior

- Any kind of physical abuse is cause to leave (No explanation needed)

With the exception of the last one, these controlling behaviors must be pervasive and have a pattern to them. You may be tempted to think that the person you suspect is, "just that way", but if they are that way *all the time*, you likely have an unhealthy narcissist on your hands. Listen to your feelings – they are a barometer of what is going on with people you interact with and inform you as to what 'feels' right and what does not.

Narcissistic Personality Disorder

Narcissistic personality disorder, or NPD, is a serious personality disorder characterized by self-centeredness, lack of empathy, and an exaggerated sense of self-importance. As with other personality disorders, this disorder is an enduring one, characterized by a persistent pattern of behavior that negatively impacts many different life areas including social, family, and work relationships. While there are plenty of other behaviors I could mention, these are all very recognizable. The diagnosis of NPD, a clinical term, is applied when a person meets all the criteria based on the Diagnostic and Statistical Manual of Mental Disorders fourth edition, DSM IV-TR.

There are many people who exhibit unhealthy narcissistic traits - from control freaks at one end of the spectrum to sociopaths at the other end. The prob-

51

lem we encounter is we cannot know the depth of their dysfunction until we encounter them and suffer the slings and arrows of their outrageous behavior! It may be verbal, emotional, physical, sexual, or a combination thereof. Here are some signs to take note of to help you identify and then take action to remove yourself from their abuse. Again, if it does not feel right, it may be time to move on.

Being Treated Like an Object

Object: Something physical that is perceived by an individual and becomes an agent for psychological identification.

Do they control what you say, how you dress, who you see, what money you have? Are you ignored? Are their opinions the "authoritive" opinion? Do they counter your opinions in front of others in a disrespectful way? Do they demean you, put you down or humiliate you in public, or private? Do they try to control what you say and to whom you speak? And do they offer no apologies for hurting you, disrespecting you, ignoring you, taunting you, or being insensitive? This is lack of empathy and indicates the N-person's inability to recognize otherness. When we recognize others we do not engage in these kinds of negatives behaviors. Healthy behavior is respecting others boundaries, treating others with courtesy, showing genuine interest in what others say and do, and reciprocating feelings and being empathic.

Being Treated Like a Servant

Servant: One that serves others, especially: one that performs duties for the person, or home of a master or personal employer.

The classic paradigm in man-woman relationships is this: the man is the main breadwinner and the woman does everything else (does most of the child-rearing, chores, cooking, and household work). These days many men are cooking and are house-husbands while many women bring home the bacon. But the unhealthy narcissist is a dependent personality, like a six- year old..... Mom, where are my tennis shoes? They know they should pickup after themselves, but don't because they expect others to do it for them. Most often they want others to support their N-environment. Same goes for the workplace. Do you work with others who expect you to pick up the slack, keep things orderly, stay overtime while they leave promptly at five every night? Do they take all the credit and pretend as if they came up with the great ideas you came up with - and then act as if you played no part? Are they dismissive or demeaning when you are alone with them, but all compliments in the presence of the boss? The bottom line here is they have no sense of fairness. In the workplace they feel entitled to all the attention garnered through achievement even though they were not the achievers! Remember, these people do not like to share and really do not understand the concept. Sharing implies equanimity and that is the opposite of domination, which is what all unhealthy narcissists prefer. BTW: These are also the co-workers who make suggestions, but do no work.

They weigh in on how things should be done, but then leave the heavy lifting for others. They always have excuses for how they are overburdened with a full agenda and rarely will volunteer for extra-duty. They are slackers and often feign competence through lack of skills. They will purposely mess up so others will make the corrections, essentially completing the work.

Lack of Intimacy

Intimacy: The condition of being intimate; close and warm.

Case studies reveal N-people can have sex and enjoy sexual pleasure, but are not able to be tender, affectionate, warm and caring. Intimacy deficiency is tied directly to the N-persons inability to empathize and recognize otherness. The N-person does not like to feel vulnerable as it creates a high level of anxiety. Their emotional range cannot perform what is required in intimacy – closeness. Plus, intimacy requires vulnerability; it requires us to open up and reveal ourselves. From the N-persons perspective, which is largely unconscious, they will not allow people to penetrate their false-mask. That might result in the false-self being exposed and others knowing their faults. Thus, intimacy is a very risky proposition for the N-person.

The Director

Director: One that supervises, controls, or manages.

The N-person is a very poor team player. Ask yourself these questions: In doing a project together, is there always a bone of contention in the mix about how to do it? Is doing tasks together does the N-person always want to direct the show (after all it's their show)? If you try to correct them, do they get very annoyed or angry, often overreacting (think tantrum)? And if they walk away, are you left doing the project? That's the Director who is always in charge. Tip: the unhealthy narcissist will not want done to them what they do to others. They will not allow others to even help them as this is interpreted as a threat. But of course, eventually others end up doing the bulk of the work at the behest of the N-person. It is seemingly contradictory. It goes like this: once they establish dominance, the N-person will direct others to complete the task at hand. But, they do not want others to offer, or initiate help as this deprives the unhealthy narcissist from setting the agenda. Once you understand that all N-persons do similar things (like setting the agenda and dominate), it gets much easier to understand their behavior.

The N-director will consistently try to manage people and too often because people on the whole want to be cooperative, the Director will get their way. This acquiescence reinforces the unhealthy narcissist's thinking - that their way is the right way. Another ploy is they will feign knowing how to do something and sucker people into helping them. So, as before, others end up doing it for them (anywhere from simple tasks to whole projects). The bottom line is others will end up having little, or no say, about most things. It is a sure sign you are dealing with an N-person when they try to direct what you do and what you say. They will even tell you to not associate with certain people, to keep secrets, limit your comings and goings, control the finances, and strip you of personal power. Many girlfriends and wives find themselves in this situation and are unable to muster the courage to break free from this dominating behavior.

The Phantom Argument

Phantom: Something elusive or delusive.

In every relationship people argue. We all have our opinions, and the truth of the matter is life is about problem solving and we all have our own approach. In a healthy relationship we work on problems and compromise and solve the problem at hand – together, respectfully. Not so with an unhealthy narcissist. They look at human interaction as competition and they like being the winner. They are very poor losers, even if the situation was not about winning or losing. The N-person sees all situations as winning or losing. In fact, they will begrudge you your own personal victories out of envy. The N-person also will provoke a situation just so they can feel superior. What's going on here?

The N-person is always managing their false-self. They use hypervigilance (watchful observation), to survey their environment. Although this self-management is largely an unconscious effort, it is important for them to feel secure and they do that through hypervigilance. If they perceive the smallest slight or criticism this will set off the phantom argument – it is defense by offense. The key to understanding the N-person is they must maintain dominance at all times. They do this in a myriad of ways, one of which is to start arguments, or provoke another person so they can mentally wrestle them to the ground. I call these *phantom arguments* as they seemingly come out of nowhere. In fact, these efforts are manifestations of the N-persons deep seated unconscious fear of being found out as being weaker than other people, so at any given time they need a dominance-fix and will provoke others to get a response and badly needed attention.

This type of behavior can be exhausting for the spouse, partner, co-worker or friend for you find you are never right in these arguments and often you will receive a verbal blow for absolutely nothing you have done, or for attempting to ward off their provocations. Narcissistic envy is a component of this damaging behavior. The N-person deep down feels inadequate and so they envy others the qualities they do not possess. It diminishes the N-person's false-self (called a narcissistic injury), when others do well or better, or if they receive a perceived slight. They cannot handle comparisons or criticisms. They are emotionally ill equipped to handle disappointments and losing. Their envy is symptomatic of repressed aggression.

Narcissistic injury definition: a blow to the fragile false-self of the N-person. The N-person often will react with rage to such an injury, real or perceived; they will lash out by devaluing, and denigrating the offender as a result.

Shame Dumping

Shame: A painful emotion caused by a strong sense of guilt, embarrassment, unworthiness, or disgrace.

This is a biggie and very important to understand. In her excellent book, *Why Is It Always About You? : The Seven Deadly Sins of Narcissism, by Sandy Hotchkiss*, shame dumping is explained. Let's take a closer look.

Shame relates to our self-image and self-esteem. When we do something good, we get approval, and we feel good about ourselves. When we do something bad, we receive disapproval, and we feel bad about ourselves. From early on, we learn what is ok and acceptable and what is not ok, or unacceptable. When in the early years of our lives our parent for the first time shows disapproval, we experience this is as shame. It's a tough lesson, up to this point we were living in a perfect little world where all our needs were being met and words were comforting, kind, and encouraging. Then we run up against reality. We do something that merits our parent's disapproval and they reprimand us. Wham! It's a blow to our undeveloped self – we experience our first narcissistic wounding. If the reprimand is followed with some soothing words and loving support afterwards, the shame of the reprimand is absorbed and handled by the child, but when the reprimand is stern and harsh and is repeated often, young children cannot handle it. The child instead will retreat into fantasy, or other psychological mechanisms to cope and "wall off", a term used by Hotchkiss, the intolerable feelings of shame. Thus, in this behavior we can find the beginnings of unhealthy narcissism. How so?

The N-person-child keeps the feeling of shame at bay. It's "over there" - away from them where it cannot touch them - where they can remain in their perfect little world free from harm. The problem with this defense mechanism is, if it persists, these children will grow up to become people who are never wrong because they never learn how to deal with shame. Consequently, to manage shame as adults, they will do something called *shame dumping*. The N-person does this by using a psychological tactic called, projection. They project onto others what they cannot tolerate in themselves. Rather than feeling their own shame for a misdeed or inadequacy, they redirect it, or dump it onto someone else. Think of it this way, the N-person's internal script is saying, "You mean, I am not perfect... you mean, I make mistakes? I cannot accept that, so it must be you to blame." Thus, shame is off-loaded as blame. Blame becomes a nasty control tactic that turns into abuse.

Here is an example. In the early days of getting to know an N-friend who was a single person, while we were having lunch one day they blatantly said to me that I was not a grateful person. I had shared with them that I was in a long-term relationship where I was not the main bread winner. They thought I had an easy life with lots of time on my hands. I replied, I was very grateful and I told them I also practiced a daily form of Sadhana (spiritual devotion), and had for many decades. I am grateful for every day I am alive and demonstrate my appreciation in many ways. Although I did not buy into their comment, it did make me feel rather sad.

What the N-person did was to dump onto me, or project onto me, their own feelings of lack about their own life and lack of gratitude for what good fortune they did have – of course, for an N-person that would never be enough. This negative commenting happened on more than one occasion. Envy was the mechanism at work here, for as with all N-persons, they envy qualities they lack and others enjoy. In the above case, they envied me for the misperception that I had more time on my hands than they did. Actually, I had very little time on my hands as I ran a consulting business, was in a longtime relationship, maintained my home, took care of my dogs, etc,. For the N-person though, it is all about perception and how these perceptions affect their false-self. Whether real or not, they will too often perceive a threat due to their own inadequacies – and being unable to handle it will dump off their uncomfortable feelings of shame onto someone else. This leaves their false-self/self-esteem intact and undamaged.

To let the reader know how I handled the sad feeling I experienced after the shame dumping episode, I did a few simple things. I took inventory of my life. I took a few days to gain some perspective through reflecting on where I was in my life, plus I did some journaling and reading. This was helpful as I realized that something more was amiss with this friendship than one simple comment or misperception. It was a series of things that had begun to happen and were starting to give me pause. Perhaps, I might be befriending someone who was neurotic, or worse, a control freak. Ironically, what I could not foresee was my journaling would reveal an unhealthy pattern of behavior that would lead to writing this book well after I ended the friendship.

No Apologies for Bad Behavior

Apology: An acknowledgment expressing regret or asking pardon for a fault or offense.

The same N-person I mentioned in the last section one day suggested I help them sabotage a neighbor's car because they had been parking too close to their designated space. I was surprised by this immature suggestion and said that it would be a bad idea and bad karma. I laughed thinking they could not be serious, but then they replied that in fact they had a can of some foul smelling stuff called *Bad Karma* and that they wanted to spray it into the air vents of their neighbor's car. I repeated myself saying it was not a good idea and that I would not do it and finally persuaded them that they should not do it. Once they saw I would not comply with their wishes, they quickly lost interest in their prank, just like a little kid would and moved quickly onto another topic. They made no apologies for their behavior of thinking to sabotage someone's property or for trying to engage me to help them do it.

It was one of a string of things like the *Bad Karma* incident which led me to seriously question the values of this person and their behavior. Eventually, after a series of successive negative encounters I disengaged from this person. The fallout led me to go on to discover that unhealthy narcissism was at work in my life not only through people like this person, but in others, like my parents.

Suffice it to say the N-person has difficulty saying they are sorry for any bad behavior as they have a woefully underdeveloped conscience. Let's piece this together. If a person cannot recognize otherness they cannot empathize. Empathy requires us to feel what others feel. Empathy is learned in our early years of development. If we are shown empathy (kindness, compassion and concern for our well-being), and we are rewarded in a positive way through reciprocation we will exhibit the same to others. If we are treated in an insensitive or abusive manner, we will have problems developing empathy and treat others in insensitive and abusive ways. Lack of empathy is a hallmark trait of an unhealthy narcissist. The N-person therefore cannot recognize when they have offended someone or when they are insensitive, or rude, or crass, or exhibit inappropriate behavior. And to add to their bag of tricks, they also know that when they do something inappropriate it garners them attention - and the N-person thrives on attention, whether appropriate or notorious. Remember, they love drama, and if there is no drama going on, they will create it. These are not the mellow types who can just hang out and relax.

What I have experienced and observed is the N-person performs and mimics behavior they know is socially acceptable, but given the opportunity will do things that are anti-social, essentially doing things their way, creating their own rules and often at the expense of others. (again, think Ponzie-scheme criminals). Anti-social behavior relegates the N-person as unique and above the crowd (meaning everybody else), and the N-person likes it that way.

Narcissistic Rage

The emotion of shame an unhealthy narcissist experiences is an intolerable feeling. Therefore, shame is offloaded as blame onto someone else. When the shame is overwhelming, the N-person will exhibit their emotion as rage. The key here is N-rage can be set off by something they perceive as a slight, and not based in actuality. An off-handed remark may be just enough to spark rage.

"Narcissistic rage is a term coined by Heinz Kohut in 1972. When the narcissist's grandiose sense of self-worth is perceivably being attacked by another person (typically in the form of criticism), the narcissist's natural reaction is to rage and pull down the self-worth of others (to make the narcissist feel superior to them). It is an attempt by the narcissist to soothe their internal pain and hostility, while at the

same time rebuilding their own self-worth. Narcissistic rage should not be confused with anger (although the two are similar), and is not necessarily caused by a situation that would typically provoke anger in an individual. Narcissistic rage also occurs when the narcissist is perceivably being prevented from accomplishing their grandiose fantasies. Narcissistic rage is frequently short-term, and passes when the narcissist rationalizes the shame that they felt."

"Kohut was the first to coin the idea of narcissistic rage. His book "The Analysis of the Self" in 1972 introduced the psychoanalytic concept as pertaining to narcissistic rage. His explanation of narcissistic rage and depression stated, "depressions are interrupted by rages because things are not going their way, because responses are not forthcoming in the way they expected and needed". He went further to say that narcissists may even search for conflict to find a way to alleviate pain or suffering."

"According to Kohut, rages are a result of the shame at being faced with failure. Narcissistic rage is the uncontrollable and unexpected anger that results from a narcissistic injury. Narcissistic injury is a threat to a narcissist's self-esteem or worth. Rage comes in many forms, but all pertain to the same important thing, revenge."

"Narcissistic rages are based on fear and will endure even after the threat is gone. To the narcissist, the rage is directed towards the person that they feel has slighted them; to other people, the rage is inco-

herent and unjust. This rage impairs their cognition, therefore impairing their judgment. During the rage they are prone to shouting, fact distortion and making groundless accusations. It is believed that narcissists have two layers of rage. The first layer of rage can be thought of as a constant anger (towards someone else), and the second layer being a self-aimed wrath. Two specific identified forms of narcissistic rage are explosive and passive-aggressive."

"The explosive form being an obvious anger, for example, damaging property (or people) and being verbally abusive. The passive-aggressive sort might be sulking or giving their target the silent treatment. They can become enraged to the point of being homicidal especially if he/she has the need to seek revenge. Narcissistic rage is usually short-term, but can provoke problems with those towards whom the anger is targeted."

Source: Wikipedia, Narcissistic rage

I have been a victim of such rage many times. It is frightening. It is an attack on your very person – your life. It is real and it is dangerous. People get restraining orders to keep these types at bay. Too often this further enrages the unhealthy narcissist as they are prevented from getting their way and blocked from further rages.

Autonomy: The condition or quality of being autonomous; independent; a state of self-determination.

If you recognize the previous pattern behaviors I have described above as something you are experiencing with someone you know, more than likely you are dealing with an unhealthy narcissist – at the very least, a control freak. The consensus on unhealthy narcissists is they generally do not improve, do not want to change, will not go to therapy, and will get worse as they get older. It is a pretty poor prognosis for them, but enough reasons for you to not stay around.

But we do stay. We stay around these people for various reasons, two being, (i) financial dependence and (ii) love. They are our spouses, our bosses, our family and friends. It can cause great hardship and upheaval to cut these people out of our lives. It is a tough personal decision. Some unhealthy narcissists are highly abusive, physically and sexually. But any kind of abuse is bad for us and simply wrong. It is a clear signal to move on. To be neglected, to be put down, to not have someone who really cares for us, to live a life of pretense is unhealthy. I believe we must take responsibility for our share of a bad "relationship" - but it does not mean we are a bad person. When attacked by an abuser, clearly the victim is not to blame.

It is a difficult decision to get out and stay out because we love these people, we care for them, we work for them, and live with them, but if we decide to move on I know one way to start - make a plan. Make a plan and set out some goals. Set out short term goals and long term goals. I think the most important one is to establish self-sufficiency. The second goal is autonomy. From those two you can do just about anything. If you have a friend to support you through your change-process that's great, but be careful because many friends are fiercely loyal to the N-person and they will turn against you.

Taking Action - The Bridge from Hope to Change

The next step after recognizing what we are dealing with is to take action. Start small, be smart and protect yourself. Here is what I suggest:

Become self-sufficient. Get a job and earn some income. Get your own checking account and save some money. Get your own car, and finally move and get your own place. If you must, get an attorney. Make sure they are well versed on unhealthy narcissism. If not, find one that is. You need a fully informed and sympathetic attorney as your ally.

You have been victimized and abused, but that is not who you are, that is what has happened to you. You are feeling diminished because you have trusted a person who is the master of deception – but they are not your master. You own yourself and your soul.

Here in the United States our way of living is based on the principles of freedom and the right to autonomy and self-determination. Many people have died for these rights. Great treatises have been written in their defense. It is our heritage to be free. We no longer serve kings or lords as servants, and no longer must we suffer the tyranny of being lorded over. Whether tyranny from without or within, we must shake off the oppression that occurs when someone tries to use us, or abuse us. So, be bold, be brave and claim your freedom.

CHAPTER 5

What is Abuse?

Power: the ability to influence change.

When I was in college my philosophy professor said those simple words one day in describing the nature of power. Those words resonated profoundly with me. With an unhealthy narcissist their whole *raison d'etre* (reason for being), is domination - having influence and power over others. When you are at the end of their control whip you will know the sting of their power. And if you become their possession, your life will become stifled and powerless.

When you feel powerless, you are not in a good place. When you feel powerless and hurt, it is time to ask yourself why? Why are you hurt, or hurting?

- Did you hurt yourself?
- Do you feel hurt due to interaction with another person?
- Did someone strike you, beat you, or force you to do something against your will?
- Did someone berate you, put you down, or bully you?

- Did someone treat you like an object through gross neglect or control tactics

Number one is not a trick question. The answer is, we hurt ourselves when we allow others to control, manipulate, or otherwise violate us in ways that are hurtful. One bad argument is not abuse - an argument that leads to violence at any level is abuse. Verbal threats and emotional intimidation is abuse. Denial of your freedom (what you think, say or do), is psychological abuse.

In order to live a healthy life, a life of well-being, we must change by changing ourselves. The next two chapters will be about how we go about that change. Before we explore those options, it is important to understand abuse and its many facets.

The first thing I want to say is this: You can change. The second thing is: You cannot change the perpetrator of your abuse. Abusive people often have been abused themselves. Research indicates abusers suffer from deep seated psychological and emotional problems that manifests in warped behaviors. Once you understand and accept that fact - that you will not be able to change your abuser - you have taken the first steps towards changing yourself and leading a healthier life.

Do you feel hurt due to interaction with another person... and/or, did someone berate you, put you down, or bully you?

As previously discussed many unhealthy narcissists are control freaks and have a big bag of control tricks. Those tricks are actually *control tactics*. Many of those tactics are subtle and covert, but many are overt and highly recognizable. What is important to understand is abusers, regardless of their personality type, use control tactics to extract compliance from others.

Emotional and Verbal Abuse Tactics:

- Intimidation
- Threats
- Put downs
- Bullying (see Chapter 11, Collective Narcissism)
- Undermining your self-esteem
- Controlling where you go, or what you say or do

As with unhealthy narcissism, abuse consists of patterns of behavior. We can all lose our temper, or say hurtful words from time to time, but when it happens repeatedly over a period of time, it is abuse. If you find that you are hurt due to being repeatedly intimidated, threatened, put down, berated or bullied, you need to recognize that you are being abused. If your self-esteem is being diminished or undermined, and if your perpetrator is trying to restrict or otherwise control where you go, or what you say or do, this is also abuse.

What to do? In my layman's opinion, if it is your boss, file a grievance. If that does not work, find another job. If it is your parent, set boundaries and use distancing as a means to lessen the instances. If it is your spouse, get counseling and legal advice, or leave. Anyone else, I would advise moving on and not seeing the person again. The use of distancing can do wonders for beginning the healing process and restoring our sense of self. Caveat: if the abuse is violent in the least, flee and never look back. There is a ton of statistics showing that physical abuse often escalates. Take heed. Many women are murdered when choosing to stay in a physically abusive relationship.

You must ask yourself a hard question: Why am I staying with an abusive person? Too often the answer is, because I love them. Here is the hard truth: that is not love - that is dependence.

It can be quite difficult to leave people we care about, more often we do not leave because we are intimidated and feel fearful. This can lead to feelings of powerlessness. Stop right there! If this is what is happening to you it is time to assess your options, summon your courage and take action. (see Chapter Six) The bottom line is to not tolerate hurtful, harmful or inappropriate behavior perpetrated against you – no exceptions!

Did someone strike you, beat you, or force you to do something against your will?

Physical abuse is a clear cut case. A person who strikes or beats you, holds you down, burns you, pushes you, or attacks you with a weapon or threatens to attack you with a weapon is a physical abuser.

Leave. Protect yourself. Seek immediate help through a shelter, police, attorney, friends or family, even your employer.

Just a sobering note: Not all unhealthy narcissists are sociopaths, but all sociopaths suffer from extreme unhealthy narcissism called malignant narcissism.

Did someone treat you like an object through gross neglect or control tactics?

If you are neglected in any key relationship, or treated like a prop or object, you are likely dealing with an unhealthy narcissist. As previously discussed, unhealthy narcissists do not recognize otherness, cannot be intimate, and have major trust issues. They are possessive of people they consider "close" or "special" but another hard truth - possession is not love. Ask yourself, do you want to be a possession?

A relationship with an unhealthy narcissist is nothing more than a non-reciprocating exercise: you give and they take, and take and take. Unhealthy narcissists do however engage in sex, but sex with an unhealthy narcissist does not translate into intimacy where warmth, caring and vulnerability are present. Let's be clear, an unhealthy narcissist may be doting and attentive, but they are either idealizing you, or you are in the early stages of the Approach-Assess-Accept-Inflate-Deflate-Devalue cycle (see Chapter One).

73

For the unhealthy narcissist you are nothing more than an extension of them – a thing, and accordingly a thing they will try to control within their environment. In addition to the above list of control tactics, I will add these with a few short notes:

Fault-finding & Criticism - You are never good enough. I hate this one as I have had my share of fault-finding and undeserved criticism simply for asserting myself. The N-person does not like when a person asserts themselves. A healthy person will assert themselves when another person challenges them, insults them, etc. The N-person will not take kindly to people who stand up for themselves or simply assert themselves. They are in charge and their need to dominate will result in verbal slights and put downs. They will one-up you on any subject, but also criticize you for being knowledgeable. Knowledge is reserved for the one who knows - the unhealthy narcissist. They love calling into question your sureness or veracity. They do this to undermine your self-confidence, to make you feel unsure and to put you off balance thus perpetuating and reaffirming to themselves their false notion as superior and most importantly, dominant.

Deflection - The unhealthy narcissist will not own up to their bad behavior. They will deflect any implication of their behavior problems using these tactics:

Contrariness - Contrariness is the equivalent to mind games. You say potato, they say, well whatever they want to say. The N-person will even contradict what they themselves have just said confusing the issue at hand. They do not like being pinned down. They must be in a one-up position all the time. That means you lose.

Minimizing - It's no big deal. Let's take bullying or put downs. It may be no big deal to the N-person, but it is for you. They will make mountains out of mole-hills and molehills out of mountains. They set the agenda. They determine what's what. It's their rules and their game.

Evasiveness - Could you be a more clear? The N-person is the master at evading direct questions and being vague. Ask them why they are late and you will receive a litany about their complicated life, traffic, someone called, etc. Often called side-stepping, they will quickly shift the focus away from themselves and onto another subject effectively obscuring the real is-sue at hand.

Diversions - The N-person will change the subject to divert attention away from taking responsibility for their own actions. You will find yourself saying, how did we get onto that subject?

Blaming - The N-person will offer up these well-turned phrases: Well, if you would only do this or that; You should have known; I could have told you that; Don't look at me, you're the one; You should have done it this way; Oh so & so, <insert your name> do you always have to; It's all your fault. They will turn the tables and soon you will be apologizing when in fact they are to blame!

Rationalization - As I have written, the N-person is always managing their false-self and thus the impression they are making on others. Kind of ironic considering they think others are mere objects. The fact is, they badly need the attention from others the quality of which can only be received from other human beings. However, they do not like being on the hook, or on the spot. One of the ways to avoid culpability is to keep others at bay through rationalization. Using this tactic the N-person is basically fighting to maintain their position as dominant rendering any social values surrounding the issue as not applying to them. They make up their own rules and will not admit culpability for any wrong action; rather they will issue various rationalizations to convince others of their reasoning conveniently excusing themselves for their inappropriate behavior.

Lies and Half-truths - It is convenient to lie and the N-person is masterful at creating lies laced with half-truths. They contain just enough of the truth to be convincing. Then again, many are just out and out liars who enjoy deceiving others. Putting one over on somebody makes them feel superior. Motive: the intent is to deceive, evade, blame or misrepresent the truth to mislead others and act in accordance with the "knowledgeable" lie put forth by the N-person.

Playing Innocent - The "who me?" tactic is one I am very familiar with in my family. Feigning ignorance is a common control tactic to avoid responsibility. It is a common defense: Gee, I did not mean to hurt you, I was not aware of, did not intend to, did not know.... blah, blah, blah.

Martyrdom - Look at all that I do for you, the N-person implies their great sacrifice, but in reality is oppressive and demanding. The implied caveat is, because of my service to you - do things my way. They have difficulty realizing (bringing into their conscious mind), that other people play a role in most of what they do in their life.

On Boundaries

This is short and sweet, but very important to understand. Good boundaries are essential to maintaining good, healthy relationships. Good boundaries means respecting others, their point of view, how they behave, what they believe in, and the choices they make. It means respecting differences. Mutual respect is the foundation for all relations in our society – it is the key element in trust. Trust fosters healthy relationships. Trust also encourages intimacy. Intimacy is the state between people that deepens the bond of love and friendship. As regards the unhealthy narcissist, the N-person has difficulties trusting others, thus they have tight boundaries, meaning they will not allow others to get close to them, but, conversely they are all over other people's boundaries. They intrude and disregard the integrity and rights of others. This means anything goes as they do not respect others because they cannot see them for who they are, and this gives them psychological license to manipulate and abuse others.

Covert Aggression

One of the best books you will ever read on control tactics is by *George Simon, PhD., titled, In Sheep's Clothing*. I highly recommend it. Dr. George Simon states that the N-person is always in a fighting mode. This fighting mode helps the N-person to maintain dominance. They are not simply defending their space, they are attacking - they are aggressing. So, think of being attacked when they use their control tactics against you. Think of a Ninja warrior in an attack stance – skilled, quick and deadly.

Conclusion

I repeat what I stated earlier… my own advice regarding people you think are unhealthy narcissists is: *Believe what they do and not what they say.* The N-person lies, deceives, betrays and otherwise will say and do whatever is needed to get you and others to do what they want. They will find fault with you as a means to dominate you. Why? Because they envy what they themselves are not, but also due to their false-self and faulty worldview of being superior they will try to dominate anyone and everyone.

Suffice it to say, the N-person leaves a trail of disappointment, destruction - and even death behind them. They fail to show up, fail to be on time, make excuses, dump on others, lack a sense of fair play, are untrustworthy and generally are unreliable. Combined with a lack of empathy and overblown sense of entitlement and it's a wonder how they survive at all. But they do survive because they make sure their needs are always met.

I have read many books by many experts and some even suggest you can lay expectations at the doorstep of an unhealthy narcissist and expect cooperation, or change. I do not agree. As the victim of abuse, I threw out my expectations a long time ago regarding abusers. The unhealthy narcissist will not change and is not motivated to change. It is not in their self-interest to do so. They have no sense of fair play, no empathy, and want to be the winner all the time. If you are in a position as an employer to fire them, or hold something over their heads they may become compliant, but the reality is they do it out self-preservation, not morality or ethics.

CHAPTER 6

Taking Action

Time to Move On

It is never an easy choice to decide to end a relationship. If the person you wish to move on from is an unhealthy narcissist though, it makes it that much more difficult. Through the first five chapters we have explored what unhealthy narcissism is, how people who are this way got this way, the nature of pattern behavior, the dynamics of how certain types of personalities feed into the unhealthy narcissist, getting out of the grasp of the unhealthy narcissist, and the nature of abuse.

The bottom line is if you persist engaging with an unhealthy narcissist you will continue to deal with being treated like a thing - objectified. I have made it plain that the N-relationship, what I describe as really a psychological dynamic, lacks two key components of fully mature and healthy relationships: reciprocation and intimacy. When one person is doing all the giving emotionally and the other is not, the giving person will eventually become energy depleted and emotionally starved for lack of those key components. If this is you, you may even find yourself in a state of exhaustion.

Understand that by choosing to stay with, or around an unhealthy narcissist, you will likely continue to endure slights, phantom arguments, undue criticism, and some form of abuse. Your life may even come under physical threat. For sure, your mental and emotional state will be under siege. Remember, unhealthy narcissism is a persistent state of being and you will not be able to change the person with this personality disorder. For all human beings, our personality is the fabric of our very being. And while it is our behavior that can be changed or modified, when dealing with an unhealthy narcissist, permanent changes to improve their behavior - meaning less controlling, more empathic and more sensitive, etc., are highly unlikely. It is simply not in their nature to do so.

So, if we choose to move on, how do we take action to improve our own life apart and away from the unhealthy narcissist?

Space and Distance

First, give yourself lots of space and keep your distance from the unhealthy narcissist. What this means is stop being drawn to the unhealthy narcissist – curb your need to be around them. Stop calling them, stop emailing, and stop being preoccupied with them. This will take some discipline because many people stay with the unhealthy narcissist because they have unhealthy self-esteem problems and/or they have a deep attachment to the unhealthy narcissist. You must break your dependence and work on breaking your own pattern behavior. Space and distance are your allies.

Now, I am not a psychologist or counselor, so you may find it of value to seek therapy or counseling during this period of important change for you. Apart from counseling or therapy though, I do know there are steps you can take which are healthy and strengthening and that I feel confident in suggesting. Ultimately, you must make your own decisions and own them – meaning take responsibility for your choices.

And this tip: do not let the psychologist set the agenda and question whether you have gotten it right about your abuser, or whether the person is in fact an abuser, or an unhealthy narcissist. The psychologist or counselor is there to help you with your next steps of getting healthy. They need to be looking forward, and not back. I have read that unfortunately many psychologists are themselves unhealthy controlling narcissists! So, do yourself a favor and do not let them play god. Find someone you think understands the subject of unhealthy narcissism and has some gut level compassion and who wants to help put you on the path to well-being.

Take Responsibility

Taking responsibility for your own choices can be difficult for the person used to having an unhealthy narcissist(s) running their lives, where the unhealthy narcissist is making all the key decisions. And the co-dependent person will likely struggle even more than others with learning to take control of their lives and changing their own behavior. Why? I have discussed in previous chapters that CDs are taught to be dependent, to be pleasers, appeasers, and acquiescent. The battle cry of the CD is: 'I can fix this!', too often meaning, I can change someone for the better. And many CDs are great at care giving and counseling and being real helpmates, but here is the reality check: When the CD tries to change an unhealthy narcissist, it is a no-go. They are dealing with a person who is recalcitrant and lacks empathy, meaning - they don't care, cannot self-reflect (will make no apologies), has impulse control problems (meaning they have addictions), and really have no motive to change to please others. In fact, that would be counter to an unhealthy narcissist's personality. Thus, the efforts of the CD are pointless. You must take responsibility for you, your life, how you live it and run it. This is part of claiming your right to be an autonomous person free from the constraints of control freaks and other unhealthy narcissists.

Accept Reality

The next step is to accept the reality that unhealthy narcissists are liars, deceivers, manipulators and controllers and to be their minion, their servant, their subordinant is simply unhealthy and more important - it is wrong. In your new play book write down and commit to memory: Do not believe what they say, only what they do. As Paul Simon says in his song, *Proof*, "Proof is the bottom line for everyone."

True to form, the unhealthy narcissist's behavior will contradict their words time and again. They may offer up convincing apologies, like the guy who batters his wife and then cries afterward and says he will never do it again, and then is good for awhile only to backslide into his old unhealthy narcissistic ways of control, domination and abuse. This is why women's shelters came into being because of this repeated pattern of abuse.

According to Washington State Office of the Attorney General, 2009 Legislative Domestic Violence Sentencing Reform:

- Repeat offenders become indifferent to legal consequences of their actions.
- The cycle of domestic violence continues unabated.
- Victims are put at greater risks due to the ineffective intervention of the criminal justice system.
- And many victims lose hope and motivation.

Here are some statistics of battered women from, *A Safe Place for Help* organization:

- 7% of women (3.9 million) are physically abused by their partners, and 37% (20.7 million) are verbally or emotionally abused.
- Every 9 seconds a woman is physically abused by her husband.
- 95% of assaults on spouses or ex-spouses are committed by men against women.

- 30% of women presenting with injuries to the emergency department had injuries caused by battering.
- From 7% to 26% of pregnant women are abused.
- 42% of murdered women are killed by their intimate partners.
- Within the last year, 7% of American women (3.9 million) who are married or living with someone as a couple were physically abused, and 37% (20.7 million) were verbally or emotionally abused by their spouse or partner. (The Commonwealth Fund, N.Y. 1991)
- Every 9 seconds a woman is physically abused by her husband. (The Commonwealth Fund, N.Y. 1991)
- The U.S. Department of Justice estimates that 95% of assaults on spouses or ex-spouses are committed by men against women. (Assessing Violent Couples, H. Douglas, Families in Society, 11/91)
- Domestic violence is a repetitive in nature: about 1 in 5 women victimized by their spouse or ex-spouse reported that they had been a victim of a series of at least 3 assaults in the last 6 months. (Bureau of Justice Statistics, 10/93)
- 30% of Women presenting with injuries to the emergency department were identified as having injuries caused by battering. (American Journal of Public Health, 1/89)
- Pregnancy is a risk factor. Several studies indicate a range of incidence from 17% to 26% of pregnant women. (Public Health Nursing, 9/87)
- 42% of murdered women are killed by their intimate partners. (FBI's 88-91 Uniform Crime Reports)

The unhealthy narcissist we are deciding to move on from may be anyone: a spouse, co-worker, boss, friend, parent, sibling, child, etc. Each of these present unique challenges on how to handle what you do when making the split. Here are some suggestions:

- Try to be respectful and not lower yourself to revenge against the unhealthy narcissist
- Try not to engage in verbal sparring to get back at the unhealthy narcissist or justify your behavior
- Try to be focused on yourself and changing your behavior and not on the unhealthy narcissist
- Create a safe place for yourself.

All of these will make you a person of integrity and not open the door for more abuse or worse, retribution from the unhealthy narcissist. If you are dealing with an extreme narcissist, never confront them! Put together a game plan, tell only your closest friend, or a family member you can trust with confidence, and move on. Do not endanger yourself by antagonizing the extreme narcissist. I have read too many times that unhealthy narcissists will take revenge and even get others to help them. They will drag you to court, strip you of your assets, lie about your reputation, stalk you, harass you at work, etc. They do not tolerate losing well and thus, my mantra: Get out and stay out and use distance as your ally.

Recovery and Rebuilding

Scenario: We have made the split. Our personal world has collapsed. Actually, it was a false world built around a person with a false-self who made false rules and used us to prop up their false world. You were living with, or befriending a person with a serious personality disorder. It will be hard to believe, but as time goes by you will come to a place where you say to yourself one day, " how did I ever get myself into something like that?" Hindsight is a sign that you are making progress and have success-fully begun distancing yourself from the unhealthy narcissist. It will be just one of many signs that you are making progress towards a healthier life.

Self-Esteem

Now, let's look at how to rebuild our esteem and lift ourselves out of the hole in which the un-healthy narcissist tossed our psychological worth.

The combination of Self Esteem + Self Confidence + Self Respect = Self Worth

Self-respect is a vital part of a person's healthy self-esteem and well-being. If you have no respect for yourself you need to begin to work on it - today. Here's how: Undo the lessons learned from the un-healthy narcissist. Being that the unhealthy narcissist cannot be empathic and they cannot reciprocate, they offered us no respect - rather they demanded subordi-nation. This undermines our self-confidence. New Re-ality: Healthy respect is a two way street. Choose to associate with people who exhibit respect for who you are and your interests. This will strengthen your self-confidence and lead to improved self-esteem. Strong self esteem produces even more confidence in oneself. Embrace confidence. Not only thinking I can do this, but I am this!

I have heard victims of abuse say," I'm smart", but they cannot seem to break away from the grip of the unhealthy narcissist. This is the power of pattern behavior that is linked to emotional dependence issues. That pattern behavior must be broken. We must practice new ways of living, thinking, feeling, behaving and being. It starts with self-respect. I am this and more! The 'more' is the power of our potential. And where there is potential there is hope for improvement and the opportunity for growth.

Set Short Term Achievable Goals

Start small. Taking small steps will help you to build upon a solid foundation of personal growth and enable you to move towards larger goals. This is called psychological work. It may be slow and go. This is not a race. Everyone heals at a different rate. Do not compare yourself to others. And as you make headway, reward yourself with your own pat on the back. Reject the "I am not good enough" script in your head that was reinforced by the unhealthy narcissist. You are good enough and always have been; now you get to be yourself and know yourself and in doing so make your claim on your life!

I want to repeat what I stated in Chapter Four: Starting small means to be smart and to protect your self. Self-sufficiency means to get a job and earn some income. Get your own checking account, save some money, get your own car, and finally move and get your own place. If you must, get an attorney – but make sure they are well versed on unhealthy narcissism.

Accept Support from Others

When a person suffers a physical injury, they seek help from those who can tend to their injury and help them heal. It is the same when we experience emotional or mental injuries. There is something called, narcissistic wounding. This is when we, anyone, experiences a blow to our self-esteem. This usually impacts our self-worth. There are a couple types of narcissistic wounding. (i) wounding to the healthy person's self; (ii) wounding to unhealthy narcissist's false-self. We will deal with the first one as this section is about healing us, the victims of abuse.

When a person has been subjected to the unhealthy narcissist's never ending judgment through criticisms, abuse, bullying, tirades, slights, and put downs, a person's ego suffers for it. This is called narcissistic wounding, one that affect's our self-esteem, self-respect and self-worth. It is important that we talk with others about our bad or negative experiences. This is not a weakness - this is seeking healing advice from friends, loved ones and counselors. You wouldn't sit around with a broken leg, so get moving to find someone who will listen and have some compassion. You may even get some good advice. The important thing is to share with a living, breathing person what you have been going through. Toss out that thinking of, "no one will understand". You deserve compassion and everyone needs empathy and understanding.

While I encourage reading books about healing and personal growth, books can take us only so far – they are a passive activity. Being proactive in our healing is necessary and rewarding. The best feeling in the world is when we receive empathy and understanding without judgment from another person. It is a balm to our bruised ego and wounded psyche.

Dump the Myth – Embrace Reality

We must learn from our mistakes, or be doomed to repeat them. This statement is so very true. The difficult reality is the N-person deceived us into believing that they loved us, were superior to us, and had our best interests at heart. That is a myth. The unhealthy narcissist contrives reality, spins words, makes stuff up, tells half-lies, and does not really live in the real world. As for love, I think unhealthy narcissists can love others, but in keeping with their unhealthy narcissism, it is an unhealthy love. They see others as possessions and things they try to control. They cannot really see people as fully fleshed out human beings. I had one say to me once, "I take care of those who belong to me." It was a scary thought.

It is an unhealthy weakness to want someone else to take care of us like a little child. As adults it is necessary that we muster the courage to confront life in all its many facets and with all its challenges. Certainly we all need comforting and caring and empathy, but do not expect those things from the unhealthy narcissist.

Grieving

I think when we lose someone (they move away, or they die, or we breakup, or they simply move on), we need to mourn their loss. It is a way to respect what has come before. Even terrible events require closure. There are countless stories of parents whose children are abducted and murdered. They insist on finding their dead child's remains so they can mourn and move on. That's what mourning does for us, it allows us to move on.

As humans, we are social creatures. We need to feel connected to others and when the fabric is torn and those we cared about are no longer to be in our lives, we can find strength and resilience in mourning. This is part of my Forward in this book. We start by forgiving ourselves and then others. We look for answers, understanding, and compassion, then we learn and we change and we grow, but in the process of all that we must take time to mourn the loss of someone who meant something to us. This gives life meaning and purpose, and it exposes us to the mystical rejuvenating power of life.

Most people we meet come into our lives but for brief moments, but there are those we cross paths with who teach us, even when the lessons are hard and the teachers are unhealthy. Compassion is a learned thing and it may be the greatest gift when we realize we are all part of the human experience. Mourning is a kind of compassion. In this case you may also be mourning your lost childhood and/or damaged psyche, and mourning the loss of a dream world that the unhealthy narcissist wanted you to believe in. Mourning will allow you to release these illusions and allow you to live according to your true self.

CHAPTER 7

Black & White Thinking

Things rarely are one way or the other - but usually somewhere in-between

I have never been much on titles, labels, or categorization. I know their function (to separate out and to define), and like many people I use them to do research, but as far as describing or defining others, I find them far too limiting.

By its nature a label tends to reduce and set apart, but when used to describe or define another person it is too often diminishing and reductive - and therein is the root of unfairness and narrow-mindedness. I prefer an open-minded approach to understanding others and believe each person's attributes are deep, wide-ranging and cannot be summed up easily. It is a great disservice we do others when we label them as it places limits on their potential, their unknown past, their unique experiences and contributions – meaning, their worth.

Our culture seems to thrive on labels: this is that, and that is this. It is a dangerous path we tread when we choose to engage in narrow-mindedness. It tends towards the type of collective thinking where whole groups of people are marginalized by others claiming superiority. The negative effects are people excluded as to civil rights, human rights, common benefits, due course of law and fair treatment; and all too often this bias is because certain differences are perceived as dangerous, debase, lesser than, or undesirable. The "not like me" syndrome is taught and learned. It is basically black and white thinking with little grey in the middle.

Cognitive Distortion is faulty thinking – logical, but not rational.

Black and white thinking is an example of cognitive distortion. It is also another trait of unhealthy narcissism where the N-person's lack of real insight into the world is based on their inability to empathize. We cannot understand one another unless we can empathize, feel what others are feeling i.e. walk a mile in my shoes. Additionally, we cannot be understood by others unless we are open and trusting. These are significant self-defeating obstacles for the unhealthy narcissist, or a narcissistic society. Life is not black and white, but a whole lot of grey in between with endless possibilities. This is what makes life so interesting and fascinating. This is what makes life rich.

Perception: process of attaining awareness or understanding of sensory information

The internal N-dialog of the unhealthy narcissist may go something like this:

- If it's not perfect, then it's useless
- If you don't love me, then you must hate me
- Either I succeed, or I am a total failure
- If I mess up this part, I may as well give up the whole thing
- If you do not agree with me, I must diminish you.

Black and white thinking is really a distorted way of perceiving the world. In the world of the unhealthy narcissist where others are objects, it is an easy way to organize their world: this goes here, that goes there. The unhealthy narcissists I have encountered often engaged in a black and white way of expressing themselves. It may be part of their constant self-image management efforts – the constant assessing what is going on in their environment and how it affects them. They arrange their life as part of their projected personality mask and ongoing inner script. Many of them are tidy perfectionists. This goes here, that goes there.... and if you are in the room with them, you will have a place too. It can be maddening. As I have mentioned before, this kind of behavior is also about control and domination. If an unhealthy narcissist can control and dominate their immediate environment they feel secure. Being that people are considered objects this means people are subject to their controlling efforts as well.

Perfectionism: There is an old maxim that goes like this: A place for everything, and everything in its place.

"Perfectionism, in psychology, is a belief that perfection can and should be attained. In its patho- logical form, perfectionism is a belief that work or output that is anything less than perfect is unaccept- able. At such levels, this is considered an unhealthy belief, and psychologists typically refer to such indi- viduals as maladaptive perfectionists."

Source: Wikipedia, Perfectionism

Unfortunately, the perfectionist has an all or nothing mindset. Black and white thinking comple- ments this type personality; it feeds into the N- person's need to have things their way in their per- fectly ordered world. As we have mentioned, they want to control everything and they will do what they need to make it so. It has been mentioned to me on more than one occasion by my mother that I have gone my own way, "you have always done what you wanted". Not quite true, but this is her perception. She is very annoyed by my autonomy (meaning I have chosen to be free from her grasp and her perfectionist expectations). However, she continues to make efforts to control me and reel me in through various ploys: passive-aggressive behavior, verbal slights, physical cues, etc. Her annoyance with me comes from her envy of my autonomy. To recap, envy for the un- healthy narcissist is a manifestation of their own feeling of their faulty grandiose false-self construct. They envy what they lack.

The unhealthy narcissist projects a perfect mask but feels imperfect; and while there is no such thing as "perfect" we can better understand their psychology by substituting the words, *whole versus not whole, complete versus incomplete.* Taking this one step further the term "un-whole" means, unsound - and unsound can mean lacking integrity. The word integrity is not always associated with morality or ethics. It also means the soundness of something, say the steel made for a car - it needs to have structural integrity. The human mind as it develops also needs a kind of structural integrity in order to mature and reach full potential. The unhealthy narcissist is stuck at an early phase of development and thus lacks the integrity (or soundness of mind), of a healthy, fully mature person with a fully developed set of emotions. Think of it as steel that has not been fully tempered. That steel will be weak and not able to withstand certain types of stress.

So, what we find are people who cannot see the full spectrum of life with its myriad of forms and ways of thinking and living. They are the ultimate victims of what the Buddha called, the illusion of duality. The illusion of duality is created by separating oneself from part or all of life – of course that is a virtual impossibility, but that is the dilemma for the unhealthy narcissist and it boxes them in to a way of perceiving the world that alienates them from family, friends and colleagues. Their unrealistic expectations cause significant dissatisfaction in relationships with other people. Their internal script does not allow for deviations or gradations in emotional context. This makes life more predictable for the N-person, (to think in black and white terms .... and to demand that things be their way), but ultimately it is unsatisfactory as it is a dictatorial way of interacting with others.

"Perfectionists can suffer anxiety and low self-esteem. Perfectionism is a risk factor for obsessive compulsive personality disorder, eating disorders, social anxiety, social phobia, workaholism, self harm, and clinical depression as well as physical problems like chronic stress, adrenal exhaustion and heart disease."

Source: Wikipedia, Perfectionism

Passive-Aggressive Behavior

To turn another person towards their way of thinking the unhealthy narcissist may exhibit passive-aggressive behavior (aggressing through passivity). Passive-aggression is a defensive behavior and also another way to control people. It is a defense mechanism which some experts believe is only partly conscious. Many experts state the passive-aggressive person is often unaware of the impact of their behavior on others. In my situation with my mother I have even commented to her to "Please do not do that..." and her response is, "Do what?" That was before my own discovery of her unhealthy narcissism. Now, I understand where it is coming from, although it really does not make it any easier to deal with her.

It is important to understand that when a person behaves in passive-aggressive ways they are aggressing against the other person. They do it through non-compliance, being politely unwilling to do something, being stubborn, feigning weakness or inability, being ambiguous, delaying decisions, or being unco-operative.

Not all passive-aggressive persons are unhealthy narcissists and vice-versa. But passive-aggression fits well with unhealthy narcissism as a means to control and intimidate others. Rather than being assertive and direct, the unhealthy narcissist will engage in subterfuge and manipulation. I would again like to refer the reader to the book, In *Sheep's Clothing, by George K. Simon*. My own approach when dealing with my mom has been to use logic when possible, and argue the point that cooperation has its benefits. For the unhealthy narcissist nearly anything that benefits them is perceived as useful. What they do not like is the equality aspect of cooperation, because then they feel they are not dominant. They always want to be one up and the other person one down.

To deal with unhealthy narcissists is a frustrating and oftentimes destructive endeavor. Press on at your own peril for they will not, and do not want to change. You must ask yourself why you are continuing to carry on with someone who you know will mistreat you, use you, has no empathy, no compassion, has no ability to carry on an intimate relationship, and will lie and deceive you. Quite frankly, once you are out of the scene they will just get somebody else to do for them what you did. That hurts, but that is the truth of the matter.

That said, I can tell you that from my point of view further self-examination of your relationship dynamics is worth the effort. It can be disturbing and ugly, but you deserve to know the truth. You might start by acknowledging that you have been a target, one among many targets at which the unhealthy narcissist aims their arrows of control. They do it to protect themselves and provide a sense of inner security. It also may help to think of them as children, but I caution against this as they are in fact, adults. The more extreme narcissists can be physically abusive and that should not be taken lightly. You will find yourself reasoning with an emotionally immature mind, though they can be quite astute mentally. Too many serial murderers are characterized as calculating and intelligent. You must also remember, they are constantly manipulating and controlling and managing their self-image - meaning the impression they make on others. But first and foremost their goals are always, themselves!

CHAPTER 8

N-Marriages & Divorce

"Take the wrong steps in divorce planning and you may lose everything: the house, the kids and your emotional stability. There is a way to take charge and keep what you want without a divorce disaster for either one of you." – Ann Bradley

This chapter will list a series of quotes by Ann Bradley, author and certified coach in Positive Psychology, and comments by me on the topic of N-marriages and N-divorces.

I have subscribed to Ann's newsletters for a couple years and she was generous in allowing me to quote from her invaluable information databank on advice for the person in an N-marriage and going through an N-divorce. I highly recommend reading her book: Divorce: the Real Truth and Hidden Dangers.

Here are some quotes from Ann Bradley's book:

- *High priced divorces and divorces amongst those 50 and over are just two of the changes in today's world of divorce. Divorce today is not like your par-*

ent's divorce. Find out what these changes are and how they make a difference in what you need to do.
■   The dangers of divorce are many and often unknown. Learn the dangers and plan ahead.
■   Divorce is not a friendly system. It is a huge industry, and divorcing a narcissist can be a difficult time especially for women who are not prepared for how bad it can be.

Bottom Line Advice from Ann:

"Because living with a narcissist can be extremely painful, it is important to understand:"

■   *You are not to blame*
■   *Narcissists ensnare everyone*
■   *Learning how to leave is important*
■   *Rebuilding a life takes courage but you can do it*
■   *There are plenty of people to help you, but it may not be your family or friends*
■   *Information can be your ally to learn you are not alone*
■   *It will take time to heal*

Also Ann writes as I have also written, *"Don't enrage the narcissist in your life. He or she will make you pay. Stay calm and plan your exit. Don't give in to 'letting it all out'. Narcissists don't forget and they like revenge. Your 'outing' of him or her adds to his narcissistic injury. A narcissist needs to look good in front of others and you gain nothing by proving he is not the best, smartest, wealthiest, most capable person he wants to be seen as."*

Are we getting somewhere yet? Yes! It is very important to understand and accept what has happened to you - and know how to take action. Shame can be debilitating. There is shame in knowing you were manipulated; the shame of knowing you were not so special but one of many that the N-person used; the shame of knowing you were even abused. Tough stuff to swallow. But, you can make it through because you now know what has happened and can self-reflect and become aware and make changes!

Remember, the N-person has a personality disorder. They have a serious problem. You got caught in a web of pure subterfuge and manipulation. It was not your fault. You trusted someone who cannot be trusted. You cared about someone who cannot reciprocate. And the time spent with these people is not a factor – meaning should not be an obstacle to moving on: one, two, five, twenty years. It's awful and the longer that you were exposed to this kind of N-behavior the more reason you have to move on.

"Life is short - and you deserve to live a good one!"

The Reinvention of You

All of this new knowledge will take time to absorb. Take the time. But also take steps to protect yourself. If you think it necessary, change your phone number, your email, even your name. You can also apply for a new Social Security number if you like. Change your habits, like shopping or eating where you and your EX shopped. You may ask why the burden is on me to do all the changing. Because they cannot, will not, and are not motivated to do so. That means you take the bull by the horns and do it – make those changes. Why else? Because as Ann says, *"You have a right to a life without fear, anger, betrayal and put downs. The part of what makes someone a victim of narcissistic abuse is not cast in stone. Flexibility is at the core of human life and the ability to reinvent one's self can be tapped into to leave the abusive situation."*

Next Steps – A Plan with Goals

"If married, a divorce without a plan could mean you end up losing custody or a home. Ask yourself, "What is my goal and how am I going to get there?" And then factor in that this is a narcissist and understand things are done differently with a narcissist."

This is about asserting your self. Your self-worth may be damaged. You may still think I am not worthy, I am stupid, I am weak. Stop! Those are lies. You must reject the scripted lies and verbal tripe that the N-person fed you. It is time to realize that you are entitled to live a quality life apart from the N-person.

In previous chapters, I suggest you do a few things. To repeat:

- Start small, be smart and protect yourself
- Become self-sufficient (i.e. get a job and earn some income)

- Get your own checking account
- Save some money
- Get your own car
- Move out and get your own place
- Use space and distance as allies
- Take responsibility for your own choices
- Accept the reality that unhealthy narcissists are deceptive – meaning they cannot be trusted
- Rebuild your self-esteem through self-reflection. Who am I?
- Set short term achievable goals
- Accept support from others
- Dump the myth – embrace reality
- Grieve and mourn the loss of your old life

If you must, get an attorney. Make sure they are well versed on unhealthy narcissism. If not, find one that is. You need a fully informed and sympathetic attorney as your ally.

Read books like Ann Bradley's on divorce. She also does counseling. Avail yourself of resources at the back of this book. Seeking help is a strength - not a weakness. Nobody does life alone – except the unhealthy narcissist.

CHAPTER 9

Celebrity Narcissism

"In a crowd, I'm afraid. Onstage, I feel safe. If I could, I would sleep on the stage. I'm serious."

On June 25, 2009, one the greatest entertainers of the music world died. His name was Michael Jackson. Known throughout the world as the King of Pop, Jackson was a brilliant dancer, singer, and businessman. His estimated worth at the time of this writing is $2 billion. He was just 50 years old.

The story of Michael Jackson is being dissected and gone over with a fine tooth comb, but what I see in the mass media blatantly is their blindness to his unhealthy narcissistic behavior. This is my opinion. I am not inclined to slander Michael Jackson, but his narcissistic profile fits like the white glove that became his trademark:

▪ He had a father who abused him physically, emotionally, verbally and psychologically.

▪ He had an overdeveloped penchant towards perfectionism; it made his performances tour de forces, but did not serve him well in his personal life. He was an overvalued child based on his innate talents. But, his own brothers encouraged and pushed him to be the front man in their band at the age of five and essentially his family turned him into a commodity – a money making machine. Here are some more traits:

- Naive and vulnerable, Michael was out of touch with others: "I hate to admit it, but I feel strange around everyday people; See, my whole life has been onstage, and the impression I get of people is applause, standing ovations and running after you. In a crowd, I'm afraid."

- The last set of traits are tied in to (i) their inability to fend off people who want to exploit them, (ii) their sense of paranoia;

- Grandiosity on an immense scale; exhibitionist; he lived a life of fantasy creating his Neverland estate, a playground estate titled after the Peter Pan fairy tale of the boy who did not age; it had a small zoo, children's rides, and the main house was designed to look like the train station at Disneyland;

- Inability to maintain intimate relationships (two failed marriages); burned through attorneys, agents, doctors, wives, associates, etc;

- Superior intellect, yet emotionally immature;

- Highly competitive: after receiving only one Grammy for his album, Off the Wall, he complained to an associate that he deserved more;

- Addictive personality; excessive acquisitiveness -- he would spend millions on things particularly gaudy, ostentatious things;

- Prescription drug abuse; a world tour had to be canceled because he checked himself into rehab; it is now known that Jackson died of a drug overdose even though he was warned specifically that drugs could kill him;

- Obsessed with his appearance; estimated perhaps fifty plastic surgeries were done on his face; he dressed in over-the- top costumes and uniforms;

- Highly protective of his reputation; was in court for allegations of child molestation and found innocent; paid off his accusers;

There may be more, but this is definitive enough. His behavior has been termed strange, but from what I see it is indicative of unhealthy narcissism. Once identified, so much could be understood. If people around him who really cared for him had known of his unhealthy narcissism perhaps they could have protected him from others who exploited him, and most importantly from himself.

Jackson's death was untimely; he was just 50 years old - young by our American standards, but for those of us who lived the life of sex, drugs, and rock n' roll in the 60s - not surprising. Many rock stars, actors, and celebrities use drugs to party, self-medicate, take the edge off, stay awake, and to sleep. It is this last one that apparently did Michael in. He suffered from severe insomnia.

I believe if we can identify unhealthy narcissistic behavior in more public figures, we may have a better chance of identifying and addressing it in our personal lives. These people need help and counseling and lots of support. Even though most unhealthy narcissists will resist such efforts, shouldn't we try? Shouldn't we try to reach out to them? As a society I think we need to take a hard look at this pervasive problem and develop ways to deal with it through new therapies, support groups and family education.

CHAPTER 10

Criminal Narcissists & Sociopaths

"He literally was the master of that situation."

I recently read where the abductor of kidnapped victim, Elizabeth Smart, has been declared a malignant narcissist. No surprise to me. Over the last year I have read about too many crimes where clearly extreme narcissism is at work.

Here is an excerpt from November 2009 Salt Lake Tribune about her abductor:

"As FBI agents interrogated Brian David Mitchell in 2003, he paused to consider his answers and carefully countered their questions about his role in the abduction of Elizabeth Smart. Videotape of the interview helped convince psychiatrist Noel Gardner that Mitchell is not psychotic or delusional but "clearly competent" to stand trial."

"He dueled with them," Gardner testified Thursday. "Even normal people would become overwhelmed. He literally was the master of that situation."

"Gardner was the first expert witness to testify for prosecutors in U.S. District Court at a hearing to determine whether Mitchell, 56, is able to understand the charges against him and assist his attorneys in his defense. The psychiatrist said the answer is simple:"

"Mr. Mitchell does not now and never has had a psychotic mental illness."

"Gardner said Mitchell has a "severe malignant narcissistic personality disorder with antisocial features" and that his selective singing and selective refusal to cooperate with his lawyers and evaluators should not be confused with mental illness."

It would be fascinating if not so terrifying. Are these people insane? No! They are extreme malignant narcissists. I mentioned mind games in earlier chapters. Mental sparring is another control tactic. Many unhealthy narcissists are quick minded and can anticipate what others will say and will verbally spar with others until they wear them down. Dialog and constructive argument is not in play. Unhealthy narcissists need to feel they are right – and more importantly that you are wrong as that makes them feel superior. As I have written repeatedly, they are masters at manipulation. They are persistent in their behavior; and looking at it from their point of view, they are defending their very being. They simply will not tolerate criticism or attacks. Dominance makes them feel secure and empowers them.

Child murderers and rapists are living through an internal scripted fantasy. It has to do with domination. The stalking is predatory, the outcome one of pure aggression. Victims are children (due to their size are easy targets), and women (due to their physical strength being less than a man is also easy prey).

You make the call. Are these people suffering from unhealthy narcissism, or worse – extreme malignant narcissism? Let's take a look.

Profile #1: Here is a crime that was an awful incident. The accused: 24-year old Raymond Clark, lab technician at Yale University. He is accused of murdering his female lab co-worker, strangling her and stuffing her body in a wall in the research lab where they both worked! According to co-workers he was known to be highly territorial about the rat cages he tended. We come to find out that he was also a major control freak and exhibited extreme possessiveness after his high school girlfriend came forward and made statements to the press about their relationship.

Profile #2: Then there is the reality television guy, Ryan Jenkins, a real estate multi-millionaire who murdered and mutilated his ex-wife and put her in a dumpster. He was later found dead from suicide in a remote motel in Canada. This guy craved attention and notoriety. He was on the reality shows, *Megan Wants a Millionaire* and *I Love Money*. He was another control freak who was highly possessive. It was reported he would go through his wife's text messages and cell phone log, Witnesses stated he hit her in public. He was also arrested for once hitting her so hard she landed in a swimming pool. His high degree of possessiveness and jealously, his need for high quality attention, and his manipulation of his deceased wife's life are examples of malignant narcissism.

Profile #3: And we cannot leave out Bernie Madoff, the notorious Ponzi-scheme criminal. He bilked friends, celebrities, charities, businesses and banks out of billions. It went on for decades and he finally stated, " It was all a lie." What you may fail to see initially is the minimization here in his glib comment? Truth be told, it was also fraud, betrayal, wholesale exploitation, immoral and highly unethical, oh yeah, and criminal - he stole the money of other trusting clients and lived the kind of life he felt entitled to without compunction.

Profile #4: The socialites and known party crashers, Tareq and Michaele Salahi, who seem so charming and benign, but in fact crashed a November 24, 2009 U.S. Presidential State dinner. As of this writing they have been subpoenaed to appear before a congressional hearing for breeching national security. Like the true unhealthy narcissists they appear to be, they have said they did nothing wrong. They see no reason to go before an investigative committee. Rather than being respectful and cooperative, the Salahi's have instead set their own agenda and are now peddling interviews for profit. They showed total disregard and disrespect for the President and his safety, yet are getting what all unhealthy narcissists want, massive amounts of attention – attention – attention!

Profile #5: Right here in my back yard of San Diego we have recently endured a horrendous murder, that of 17 year old Chelsea King. Here is a description of her murderer, John Gardner III, in the San Diego Tribune newspaper:

"He shoveled snow and carried groceries for a neighbor. He cared for a sick girlfriend by pressing a cool cloth to her head all afternoon. A former high school girlfriend called him "the one person who has made me feel completely safe in this world."... Gardner, who pleaded not guilty Wednesday to murder and assault with intent to commit rape, was linked to King's death from semen found in the victim's clothing, said California Department of Justice of spokesman, Christine Gasparac.... A court-appointed psychiatrist, Dr. Matthew Carroll, urged the "maximum sentence allowed by law" in 2000 for Gardner for molesting a 13-year-old neighbor at his home, according to court documents. He called him "an extremely poor candidate" for treatment because he refused to admit any responsibility."

There are literally boatloads of these people popping up everyday in the press. They are wanton, notorious, dangerous, deceptive people perpetrating a whole range of crimes: security breeches, larceny, fraud, kidnapping, robbery, home invasions, assault (beatings and rape), and murder.

The fact is, extreme narcissism is not to be taken lightly. It is another warning that I feel I must make to my readers: you cannot manage relationships with these people. They set their own agenda. They play and live by their own rules – it is fantasyland and horror all wrapped together. And from where I sit, the charming Salahi's are nearly as bad as the N-murderers for they put the President of the United States (and therefore our country), at dangerous risk by demonstrating wholesale disregard for national security protocol. BTW: They were also involved with another reality show. Attention – attention – attention.

The bottom line is the core element lacking in any sociopath is empathy. They simply do not care. If a person does not care, they will not respect others or play by societies' rules or laws. It is well known among psychiatrists who size up sociopaths that children who later become sociopaths exhibit warning signs. They lack empathy, hurt animals, are highly manipulative, and insist on getting their way. In making their own rules they feel entitled to do as they please without restriction. As adults, they have no moral compass and thus engage in criminal or unethical behavior without remorse. As with most unhealthy narcissists they have underdeveloped emotions, lie, con, engage in addictive behaviors, have little impulse control, are irresponsible, unreliable, and exhibit superficial charm to hoodwink others. They are despicable characters in everyway and very dangerous as they have no moral center. This is why I have stated that you do not know the depth of their dysfunction and this is exactly the reason to disengage from interacting with extreme unhealthy narcissists.

CHAPTER 11

Collective Narcissism & Our Future

"Our task must be to free ourselves by widening our circle of compassion to embrace all living creatures and the whole of nature and its beauty."

I try to live my life accordingly, and like Albert Einstein, whose quote above encapsulates my own sentiments, I believe that by further developing my compassion I am a better human being. I am more able to empathize and be sympathetic to the suffering of others. I am more conscientious and respectful of nature and all its wondrous creatures. I am better able to separate out that which is trivial and that which is of value.

"The high destiny of the individual is to serve rather than to rule."

This quote by Einstein is parallel to the nature of the plot in Hermann Hesse's seminal work, *The Glass Bead Game*, a book about one man's life in the 25th century, a man who is dedicated to the intellectual pursuit of mastering a complex game, the Glass Bead Game - a synthesis of mathematics, music and cultural history. Upon achieving the highest rank as Magister Ludi (master of the game), after years of study and practice, he experiences a crisis of conscience, one that leads him to an epiphany – that as adept as he was in his scholarly pursuits and achievements, he had misunderstood the real purpose of life – to be of service to others for the common good, to share knowledge, and care for others. In 1946 Hesse received the Nobel Prize for Literature for the *Glass Bead Game*.

Another powerful and insightful quote by Einstein which fits nicely with the lesson of the Glass Bead game is, "Try not to become a man of success, but rather try to become a man of value."

While many unhealthy narcissists are busy achieving fame, notoriety, status or even infamy, there are other people with healthy psyches and personalities busy in these same pursuits. Is it a crime to be famous? No. Or achieve status? No. But, in the final analysis of what our life means and what our legacy will be, what is abundantly clear is that what has real value is very much the opposite.

Personal fulfillment comes from enjoying the passage of time, taking pleasure in the ordinary, being who we are, and caring for others in a kind and compassionate way. Unlike books who tout secrets or esoteric knowledge, I am writing to convey the obvious. Choosing self-lessness over self-interest is the lesson to be learned. It may take a lifetime, or it may be understood quite easily, but I think once understood it is something that we must practice everyday. By doing so, we develop an aesthetic view towards life. For me that aesthetic is following the good, the true and the beautiful. Mere ideals? Not at all. I am interested in doing good works, being a good person, and treating others with respect. I am interested in true knowledge, integrity, and living in accord with nature. And lastly, the beautiful, that which life is in all its many facets is what sustains me, it fuels my artistic and creative life, it is what I love most about being alive.

Societal Wants, Needs, and Entitlement

Currently modern societies are not living in accord with nature and they are not practicing integrity of values. In fact, they are denying true knowledge – the fact that our planet is in trouble. The future of the ecology of our planet hinges on humanity reigning in its entitlement behaviors and developing empathy not only for our fellow man, but for all the creatures and life who share this Earth. The persistence of human entitlement behavior is damaging our ecosystem plain and simple. Exploitation of our common resources is having catastrophic effects on our land, our rivers, our oceans, our forests, our atmosphere, plus the animals, fish, birds and even the bees that inhabit our Earth. Even if you do not agree that there is global warming, there are countless other concrete examples of extreme damage from mountain top blasting to coral reefs dying; from irreversible species annilhation to the poisoning of our scarce fresh water resources.

"November 2009: According to the International Union for Conservation of Nature more than 17,000 species are endangered. The Switzerland-based group surveyed 47,677 animals and plants for this year's "Red List" of endangered species, determining that 17,291 of them are at risk of extinction."

"More than one in five of all known mammals, over a quarter of reptiles and 70 percent of plants are under threat, according to the survey, which featured over 2,800 new species compared with 2008."

"March 2010: The practice of "fracking", natural gas drilling where large water sources in multiple states are being poisoned throughout the United States was exposed in a new film by Josh Fox called, Gasland."

There are a whole host of stories documenting fresh water shortage, but let's face it – we are experiencing the wholesale breakdown of our life sustaining eco-system through overuse, negligence, irresponsible use, and blatant exploitation. This reality challenges us to make serious changes that can come only from reflecting upon what we have been doing individually and collectively. We must take account of our societal actions. But we cannot wait for "others" to do it. We cannot wait for our government to do the right thing. We, as individuals, must do it. And I believe by changing ourselves, abandoning unhealthy entitlement behavior, we can create new ways to exist and thrive. We can and must restore the health of our planet. If we choose to persist in our own unhealthy pattern of collective selfish behavior, we will experience catastrophic results.

Water – The Tie That Binds

According to National Geographic, April 2010, " Nearly 70% of the world's fresh water is locked in ice." The rest is in aquifers that we are draining faster than nature can replenish. "Two thirds of our water is used to grow food. With 83 million more people on Earth each year, water demand will keep going up unless we change how we use it." Indeed, the lack of fresh water will mean crop failure. Herds and flocks will be subject to water restrictions and decline. Damage to fisheries will exacerbate the problem. Mass starvation will escalate. Decline in manufacturing due to lack of water will accelerate job loss and economic output. Water wars will be inevitable.

Exaggeration? Right now in California we have an ongoing fight between the Federal Government mandating reduction of water use to save a fish species, the Delta Smelt, and farmers who use the same waterway in the Sacramento-San Joaquin Estuary for irrigating their crops. Who is right and who is wrong? If we continue to sacrifice species we will continue degrading our ecosystem. Our Chinook salmon industry is already on its back. On the other hand, if we cut water supplies to farmers we will grow fewer crops and produce prices will go up. It is important to understand a couple things: once a species is lost, it is gone forever – permanently. We can always grow more almonds. We cannot create more species of fish. Contrary to those with the God-complex, we are not God. We can save these species because there are solutions. Encouraging statewide rainwater recapture would alleviate residential demand and help farmers in dry years. But, we must be willing to change our patterns of behavior to make it work. Rather than looking out for our self-interest where win-lose is the outcome, we need to find collaborative win-win solutions. Common interest over self-interest ultimately will yield benefits for each person.

FYI: As my book is going to press, here is an update from the Fresno Bee on the Delta Smelt:

"March 31, 2010 Sacramento-San Joaquin Delta pumps will be ratcheted back today after a federal judge in Fresno rejected a request to keep them operating temporarily at current levels.

Wednesday's ruling by U.S. District Judge Oliver W. Wanger, means that for the next two months, both the federal and state water pumps will move much less water to users, including the Westlands Water District and the Metropolitan Water District of Southern California.

It's the latest loss for farmers and other water users in the decades-long battle over moving water through the state. That battle continues today when water users and environmentalists square off in Wanger's court in what promises to be a pivotal case.

*The seasonal cutbacks that Wednesday's rul-
ing allows, are part of a controversial management
plan for endangered spring-run Chinook salmon and
Central Valley steelhead. Authorities say the pumps
endanger juvenile fish heading out to the Pacific
Ocean."*

Collective Action

Part of taking action (as described in Chapter
Six for separating ourselves from unhealthy narcissists), is not so different from what can be done collectively to separate ourselves from broad social unhealthy narcissistic behaviors. Meaning... it can bene-
fit every single one of us to consciously choose the
path of self-lessness over egocentric self-interest. Unfortunately, the habit of many people is to forget about
other people's needs when all their own needs are being met. When I am in my recliner watching my favorite television show, I am not usually thinking about
global warming. When I am driving around doing er-
rands with a full tank of gas, I am not thinking about
how we have reached the *peak oil* era. When my refrigerator is full, I am not really focused on global
hunger. I think I have made my point, but the reality is
that it is so easy to become rather indifferent to our
fellow man and to the worlds suffering when our core
needs are pretty much met.

How Can We Get Better?

American psychologist, Abraham Maslow, put forth the concept of *self-actualization*. Maslow believed humans have a natural tendency towards achieving healthiness, or self actualization. Maslow created a visual aid to explain his theory, the Hierarchy of Needs. It is a pyramid depicting the levels of human needs, psychological and physical. When a human being ascends the steps of the pyramid he reaches self-actualization.

- Basic Needs - At the bottom of the pyramid are the "Basic needs" of a human being, food and water and touch.
- Security and Stability - These two steps are important to the physical survival of the person. Once individuals have basic nutrition, shelter and safety they attempt to accomplish more.
- Love and Belonging – these two are social needs; when individuals have taken care of themselves physically, they are ready to share themselves with others.
- Esteem - The fourth level is achieved when individuals feel comfortable with what they have accomplished. This is the "Esteem" level, the level of success and status.
- Self-actualization - occurs when individuals reach a state of harmony and understanding.

"Maslow based his study on historical figures, including Albert Einstein, as well as people he knew who clearly met the standard of self actualization.

123

Maslow used Einstein's writings and accomplishments to exemplify the characteristics of the self actualized person. He realized that all the individuals he studied had similar personality traits. All were "reality centered," able to differentiate what was fraudulent from what was genuine. They were also "problem centered," meaning that they treated life's difficulties as problems that demanded solutions. These individuals also were comfortable being alone and had healthy personal relationships. They had only a few close friends and family rather than a large number of shallow relationships. One historical figure Maslow found to be helpful in his journey to understanding self actualization was Lao Tzu, The Father of Taoism. The basis of Taoism is that people do not obtain personal meaning or pleasure by seeking material possessions."

"Maslow argued, the way in which essential needs are fulfilled is just as important as the needs themselves. Together, these define the human experience. To the extent a person finds cooperative social fulfillment, he establishes meaningful relationships with other people and the larger world. In other words, he establishes meaningful connections to an external reality--an essential component of self-actualization. In contrast, to the extent that vital needs find selfish and competitive fulfillment, a person acquires hostile emotions and limited external relationships--his awareness remains internal and limited."

Source: Wikipedia, Abraham Maslow; Hierarchy of Needs

I embraced Maslow's theories when I was nineteen during my first year as a psychology major. For me, the keys to the kingdom are stated above. Cooperation over competition is the path to well-being, both personal and collective. In the modern western world we are in a constant state of competition: we compete for money, jobs, resources, homes, parking, even driving space on the roads and freeways. We jostle at the airport and the shopping centers and the grocery stores. We compete for the best bargains. And trying to find some private space to rest and relax is near impossible for we even have to compete for recreational space. I live in Southern California where the beaches tend to always be full of people. On holidays the attendance can reach upwards to a million! Living in a near constant state of competition is a complete drain on our adrenal system and counter to overall health. This is just one more reason why we need to get on the path to well-being. Overstressing our bodies can only lead to a decline in health and quality of life.

Maslow generalized that among other things, self-actualizing people tend to focus on problems outside themselves; they have a clear sense of what is true and what is phony; they are spontaneous and creative; and are not bound too strictly by social conventions.

For those of us who progress and become healthier on our path to well-being we must also develop compassion for others. At some time in our lives we will become reliant on others to help us, to do for us, to heal us, and help us. Think, pay it forward. Make a down payment on the future by becoming an actively caring person today. Doing good, has its own rewards – it makes us feel good. It is a noble expression when we take our personal responsibility seriously and not only to help others but to reduce our consumption of natural resources. Why? Because we all share what is available - and what is available is limited.

The Big Con

The book, *The Secret*, by Rhonda Byrne, was recently released encouraging people to get what they are entitled to through attracting what they want. Want a new car? Attract it. New house? Just think about it in the "right" way and attract it. This clever book is based on false psychology. In fact, what it is tapping into is something called, magical thinking.

"In anthropology, psychology, and cognitive science, the term 'magical thinking' is used to describe causal reasoning that accords unwarranted weight to correlation or coincidence. It often includes such ideas as the ability of the mind to affect the physical world."*

It is a false notion and assumption that if I do this, then that will happen - even though I have no idea how it is caused, or why. The gurus of the new, *self-help-yourself to everything philosophy* tweaked this notion by providing a bogus cause – the law of attraction. They also slicked up the marketing with a

DVD video that had all kinds of vague esoteric knowledge laced in between with new age music and had expert self-help gurus commenting over the visuals. I doubt they marketed this to Botswana or the Aleuts. No, they chose the hub of materialism – the United States. They hit their target market and the DVD rang up $65 million dollars in sales. In 2007, the book sold more than 4 million copies.

*"Wishful thinking is the formation of beliefs and making decisions according to what might be pleasing to imagine instead of by appealing to evidence or rationality."**

Source: Wikipedia, Magical Thinking

Actually, the people who promote this type of thinking are messing with people's sense of reality. They conveniently swap out words like attraction where the words should be wishing thinking. Wishful thinking and magical thinking are the same. You can hope and pray and wish for something you want to happen, but that does not mean it will happen. Hoping and praying and wishing can all be positive things to do, to help us feel like we have some sense of control in situations where we have none. But seriously, we need to get our expectations in line with reality. To get the things we want, to achieve our goals, we must plan, have the means and motivation, and then act. Even in small daily events, like grocery shopping, we must decide when we are going to go, what route we will take, what we will buy and how much we can spend. Then we have to get into the car and go do it! I cannot attract the groceries to magically arrive at my house in my refrigerator!

The power of the book, *The Secret*, taps into times when we are unhappy or depressed, when things are not going right, or as we wish them to be. This opens the door to magical thinking – this is actual psychology. The target is the motivation part of the equation. They are saying that people just are not thinking right. If you buy the book and learn the "secret", and learn to think correctly, the world is your oyster. That is pure fantasy.

What's the Harm?

The Secret implies there are no limits to what can be acquired. It claims our big hang up is we mistakenly think that there is not enough to go around. So, the conclusion is we suffer from negative thinking. If only we could avail ourselves of the secret law of attraction we too could access the keys to wealth building, the perfect partner, a beautiful house, the great body we desire and anything else. They posit that thought=creation. This kind of thinking had to have hooked every unhealthy narcissist who read this stuff. All you with the God-complex line up here for your copy. Grandiosity fantasies fulfilled!

The Secret also implies that the world has limitless resources. That's a lie. The world is finite and made with a limited amount of everything. Back down to reality. People with a sense of proportion consume to fill a real need: food, shelter, clothing, sundries, car, fuel, etc. People who want-want-want, and consume-consume-consume, do so for very different reasons - to fill a psychological-emotional need. They do it because it makes them feel better. Better about what? It is their lack of fulfillment.

The solution to addictive consumption is all wrong. This type of need cannot be filled by what can be bought, possessed or manipulated. It is a psychological need to be validated, to be loved, acknowledged and appreciated; to know that our existence matters. We can be fulfilled by living a life that has purpose, integrity, and real worth. If parental acknowledgement was not present, or faulty in a person's life, that person will seek other ways to receive attention or approval – meaning through gratification. Many of those paths of gratification are unhealthy, indicative of the person's underlying personality problems. When we believe we are entitled to everything that our heart desires we are not living in reality. When extreme narcissists with extreme needs take over countries and inflict their extreme needs upon the world we have seen what happens – wars, conflict, and suffering. Where extreme narcissism rules, deprivation and destruction follows.

For Your Own Good

I shun the name, Hitler, because for my parents generation, he was evil incarnate. During their young lives and the years they spent at war in World War II, Hitler was the essence of evil. I read William Shirer's powerful book, The Rise and Fall of the Third

Reich, when I was twelve. It stunned me. I was shocked to learn of the atrocities and cruel behavior perpetrated by the Nazis and those who followed and allied themselves with them. It was the ultimate history lesson on despotism.

While researching unhealthy narcissism I read several books and articles by the well-regarded Swiss psychoanalyst, Alice Miller. Her focus has been on how a damaged childhood can be the source of psychopathic violence. She was ten years old and living in Berlin when Hitler came to power. She became interested in understanding how civilized people could follow a "primitive" and "arrogant monster" like Hitler. The key lay in Hitler's upbringing. As Miller has, I myself have read where Hitler as a young boy endured severe beatings on a regular basis. He would be awoken out of the safety of his bed in the middle of the night by another monster, an alcoholic father who would beat him without remorse.

Societies that tolerate such parental behavior and allow children to be beaten as a part of their authoritarian societal structure are setting the stage for persons like Hitler to rise to power. Those societies are full of adults who as children were taught to defer to authoritarian rule with absolute obedience. In the case of pre-WWII Germany, what happened in the home transferred to the greater society. It is easy to draw the link in absolutist extreme narcissistic thinking that "might makes right" and blind obedience will be rewarded.

I highly recommend Alice Miller's excellent book, *For Their Own Good*, as it will introduce you to social narcissism and how it gets a foothold in otherwise civilized societies.

Op-Ed Will Not Help Planet Earth

We are living in an age where everybody has an opinion – whether it is based in fact or not, is another matter. Op-ed journalism rules the airwaves. YouTube™ thrives on breaking news but also spews junk in high volume. Blogs on a myriad of subjects and loaded with every kind of opinion are in ever growing numbers filling the servers of the Internet across the globe. The sheer weight of it all is bound to crash the Internet at some point. My own work for this book is based on one steady year of reading, studying and researching the topic of unhealthy narcissism and another two years of continued study and research. That first year I spent every day reading relevant material. I am now well versed in the subject at hand. I have to say I loathe the poorly researched newspaper articles I see appearing too often these days and then reprinted over and over in other news media, including blogs and social networks so that in its repetition fiction becomes fact - the preposterous becomes credible. This sort of journalism is detrimental to our society.

What I do know is this: perpetuating false-arguments and false data about serious problems, like climate change, will lead any society down the road to ruin. When false-arguments and false data is purposely promulgated by authorities it is propaganda. Free societies steer clear of such dangerous tripe and defend against such use of information. It is no surprise then that Hitler, a malignant narcissist along with his sociopathic henchmen, used carefully crafted propaganda to manipulate the masses and reinforce their self-delusion of a pure Aryan race and an apocalyptic belief of a thousand year reign. The purpose, and or consequence of propaganda, half truths, is to make something that is really only a belief appear to be knowledge, or a truthful statement to represent the whole truth, or possibly lead to a false conclusion. This is how whole societies can jump on board and support a fascistic state. Does this sound familiar? The half-lie laced with half-truth? Unhealthy and extreme narcissism can develop into social and collective narcissism where whole nations will exhibit the traits of entitlement, grandiosity, lack of empathy, need for admiration, and arrogant, haughty behaviors. That is a bull's-eye when describing many modern industrialized countries today.

Water on Planet Earth

So this leads us back to today problems in the world and the very real global problems facing us – the human race. Let's look again at the most critical resource: water. Every living thing has a stake in water on our planet. The whole of humanity, every creature, every plant, every blade of grass and stalk of grain depends on water to exist. No water – no life on planet Earth. Less water – less life. It is the point in between those two that is of greatest concern. When there is not enough water, wars break out, people will thieve water from wells and from aquifers. People will kill for water. I am not talking about what might happen or history, but what is happening now.

For more information go to: World Water Wars: http://www.worldwaterwars.com

Here is some statistical information from Water.org:

"Nearly one billion people – about one in eight – lack access to clean water. More than twice that many, 2.5 billion people, don't have access to a toilet. Only 2.53 percent of earth's water is fresh, and some two-thirds of that is locked up in glaciers and permanent snow cover. But despite the very real danger of future global water shortages, for the vast majority of the nearly one billion people without safe drinking water, today's water crisis is not an issue of scarcity, but of access."

- *3.575 million people die each year from water-related disease.*
- *43% of water-related deaths are due to diarrhea.*
- *84% of water-related deaths are in children ages 0 – 14.*
- *98% of water-related deaths occur in the developing world.*
- *884 million people, lack access to safe water supplies, approximately one in eight people.*
- *The water and sanitation crisis claims more lives through disease than any war claims through guns.*

- *At any given time, half of the world's hospital beds are occupied by patients suffering from a water-related disease.*
- *Less than 1% of the world's fresh water (or about 0.007% of all water on earth) is readily accessible for direct human use.*
- *An American taking a five-minute shower uses more water than the typical person living in a developing country slum uses in a whole day.*
- *About a third of people without access to an improved water source live on less than $1 a day. More than two thirds of people without an improved water source live on less than $2 a day.*
- *Poor people living in the slums often pay 5-10 times more per liter of water than wealthy people living in the same city.*
- *Without food a person can live for weeks, but without water you can expect to live only a few days.*
- *The daily requirement for sanitation, bathing, and cooking needs, as well as for assuring survival, is about 13.2 gallons per person.*
- *Over 50 percent of all water projects fail and less than five percent of projects are visited, and far less than one percent have any longer-term monitoring.*

You may find Vandana Shiva, a leader in the International Forum on Globalization and who has written many compelling books, an interesting author. Her book, Water Wars: Privatization, Pollution, and Profit, is a real eye opener.

The New York Times reported in 2004: "Make no mistake, what's happening to the glaciers in Tibet is happening around the globe," said Dr. Lonnie G. Thompson, a professor of geological science at Ohio State. "Our measurements show that between 1850 and 1960, the glaciers retreated 7.5 percent. Between 1960 and 2000, there was a further 7 percent retreat. In the 1990's alone, the glaciers have shrunk by more than 4 percent."

You can view the global glacier melt on National Geographic web site under the link, Global Retreat. The map shows major glacier melt which feed river systems. Once melted those river systems will dry up. Countries like China and India will be severely impacted.

They also have an excellent piece called, The Big Melt and Six Degrees Could Change the World. Climate Progress.org posted an article February, 2009 entitled, M.I.T. Joins Climate Realists where they state,:

"The MIT Integrated Global System Model is used to make probabilistic projections of climate change from 1861 to 2100. Since the model's first projections were published in 2003 substantial improvements have been made to the model and improved estimates of the probability distributions of uncertain input parameters have become available. The new projections are considerably warmer than the 2003 projections, e.g., the median surface warming in 2091 to 2100 is 5.1°C compared to 2.4°C in the earlier study."

So, what kind of a world will be living in when millions upon millions are left without water? Some would say, better off as populations will decline. That could only be the sentiment of a heartless, self-centered person. To think that what happens a continent away will not have consequences here in our own country is naïve at best. Countries are all tied together through international trade and commerce. Catastrophes of this magnitude will have devastating effects on the world stage. The destabilization of world economies will likely lead to more wars and more unrest; more illness and more suffering. The clock is ticking and the window of opportunity is closing. If we continue to listen to politicians who are serving their own self-interest by serving the interests of the large corporations and banks and multi-nationals over the interests of the American people and its future, we are doomed to a frightful future.

As free people we need to reclaim our destiny and free ourselves from the clutches of collective narcissism. As with understanding unhealthy narcissism on a personal level, we need to bring ourselves up to speed on what is actually taking place in our world under the influence of collective narcissism. Multinational corporations who are bypassing legislative regulation are wreaking havoc not only on our planet but on our economies as evidenced by the 2008 global credit markets collapse. These same companies are influencing governments to wage wars for profit. They are also the major polluters across the globe. When is enough, enough?

As I was writing this book, the global economic collapse occurred. It was not too difficult to see the connection between collective narcissism and the self-serving interests of large corporations and multinational companies who are involved in nefarious practices. Accordingly, I have started writing another book about collective narcissism and its negative affects on our modern societies. I cannot stand idly by while I watch our natural resources be polluted, strip-mined, overused, and exploited. I can no longer abide the lies I hear everyday in our media reports that mislead the public about climate change. It is not enough to improve our own personal lot in life. We have a moral duty, or as Rousseau stated and Jefferson agreed, a social contract to fulfill.

"MAN is born free; and everywhere he is in chains. One thinks himself the master of others, and still remains a greater slave than they. How did this change come about? I do not know. What can make it legitimate? That question I think I can answer."

"If I took into account only force, and the effects derived from it, I should say: "As long as a people is compelled to obey, and obeys, it does well; as soon as it can shake off the yoke, and shakes it off, it does still better; for, regaining its liberty by the same right as took it away, either it is justified in resuming it, or there was no justification for those who took it away."

"The problem is to find a form of association which will defend and protect with the whole common

137

force the person and goods of each associate, and in which each, while uniting himself with all, may still obey himself alone, and remain as free as before."

Source: Constitution Society

CHAPTER 12

Well-Being

There is life after the unhealthy narcissist – it is called well-being.

I started studying different ways of thinking, living and being when I was very young. It has been my saving grace. I chose to be curious, to look outside my own family and beyond the religion in which I was raised. I trusted my inner instincts and embraced all different kinds of knowledge. It is not easy to discover that ones' family is dysfunctional. It is harder still to accept that unhealthy narcissism was at the root of the dysfunction. It saddens me because I know these people will never change. It saddens me even more because I know there will never be any healthy love between us.

What I have chosen to do is heal myself and try to help others by writing this book. I have taken my own co-dependence and transformed it into real compassion. While there are hundreds of books on personal growth and thousands on psychology, I offer up this simple statement by the Buddha, "Find your own salvation." It is truly the thing that an abused or exploited person must do – save themselves from those who would oppress and hurt them. Look to God, look to the heavens, walk in nature, commune with something bigger than what you are and you will find answers. You will find that you have a place and a purpose and that you have value. Your life means something. It may be different from what others have told you or it may lead you back to where you started. The journey is worth the effort.

And just as there are thousands of books and articles and helpful advice and spirit guides, etc., the road is not defined. It will be in this undefined way that you will find the path back to your self. Ponder these quotes to help you along your way:

"Before you embark on any path ask the question: Does this path have a heart? If the answer is no, you will know it, and then you must choose another path. The trouble is nobody asks the question; and when a man finally realizes that he has taken a path without a heart, the path is ready to kill him. At that point very few men can stop to deliberate, and leave the path. A path without a heart is never enjoyable. You have to work hard even to take it. On the other hand, a path with heart is easy; it does not make you work at liking it."

"Anything is one of a million paths. Therefore you must always keep in mind that a path is only a path; if you feel you should not follow it, you must not stay with it under any conditions. To have such clarity you must lead a disciplined life. Only then will you know that any path is only a path and there is no af-front, to oneself or to others, in dropping it if that is

what your heart tells you to do. But your decision to keep on the path or to leave it must be free of fear or ambition. I warn you. Look at every path closely and deliberately. Try it as many times as you think necessary."

"This question is one that only a very old man asks. Does this path have a heart? All paths are the same: they lead nowhere. They are paths going through the bush, or into the bush. In my own life I could say I have traversed long, long paths, but I am not anywhere. Does this path have a heart? If it does, the path is good; if it doesn't, it is of no use. Both paths lead nowhere; but one has a heart, the other doesn't. One makes for a joyful journey; as long as you follow it, you are one with it. The other will make you curse your life. One makes you strong; the other weakens you." The Teachings of Don Juan by Carlos Castaneda

Here is wishing you a joyful journey.

Afterward

The destructive behavior of bullying is manifesting itself all too often these days. I have not heard a single news outlet mention unhealthy narcissism as part of the reason behind bullying. Entitlement is what drives bullying – the unhealthy narcissists' need to feel superior to prop up their false-self. This drives them to treat others as inferior. Collective narcissism was at work in a recent report of a high school student, a young woman, who was bullied relentlessly to the point where she committed suicide. They broke down her defenses, her self-esteem, and ultimately her self-worth. They effectively destroyed this person's sense of self. No doubt, there was a primary N-person who employed others to follow their lead in these attacks - it was pure collective narcissism.

As with Emil Sinclair in *Demian*, victims of bullying need other healthy people to help free them from the bully. A game-changer needs to be introduced into the situation to interrupt the cycle of destructive behavior of the offending unhealthy narcissist. The game-changer in this case needed to be someone who would have had authority over the bully: a principal who can suspend the bully would have been ideal. The police should have been called and they should have sent a community police officer to the home of the bully/bullies to warn them of possible charges and criminal consequences. I have read that most unhealthy narcissists will submit to authority. The ones who do not respect authority and will not change their behavior will need other methods to be employed to get their attention and make them change. When a controller or bully bypasses authority and impinges on the common decency and civil rights of others, we must act! Parents, community leaders and local enforcement do not get a pass for not intervening to protect other from being bullied. In fact, it should be a rallying cry – a call to action.

I have been bullied and only recently was on the receiving end of verbal bullying. While space and distance are my allies, I may have to change my email address. For the time being, I blocked the offenders email address. I also shared the incident with a friend who knows me so that someone else was aware of the bullying. I will have no more contact with the offender. Unlike me though, the high school student could not free themselves from their environment, thus they were very vulnerable to daily incidences of bullying from this group of N-abusers. In my opinion, the parent, who was aware of the situation, should have removed their child from the school and then retained an attorney. I would have brought in all authoritive parties to quell the violence against this person.

No one is entitled to make themselves feel better at the expense of others. I hear self-help gurus state that we all deserve to feel good about ourselves, but what they do not take into consideration is that we must also address entitlement behavior, and in particular unhealthy narcissistic entitlement behavior, when making such blanket statements. We must keep in perspective what values we are teaching when promoting self-improvement. We must encourage civil discourse and dissuade others from base humor and judgmental tirades. Our mass media unfortunately promotes this sort of negative rhetoric. Everyday we see politicians and talking heads go at each others throats. It is despicable. It is disgraceful behavior and demeans our democracy in a great country such as ours. The bottom line is taking advantage of the weak and exploiting those who cannot fend for themselves is wrong. Pigeon-holing is narrow-minded. Exploiting anyone shows a defect in character. People have different attributes, abilities, aspects, traits, cultural heritage, opinions, beliefs, and ways of living. Teaching tolerance and respect for others will yield a more peaceful, positive, and productive society.

The N-person who prompted the writing of this book and who is also a parent, one day made an awful joke. We were driving in their car and they read aloud the bumper sticker on the car ahead of us. It was one that is very common: My child is an honor student at such-an-such school. The N-person then said, "Yeah, well I would like to see a bumper sticker that said: *my kid beat up your kid at such-an-such school.*" And then they laughed out loud at their own twisted humor. My thought at the time was one of being appalled. It was off-putting. It was also a dead giveaway that their projected personality was fake. Here was a person who would talk about new age ideals in one breath and then make such negative statements like that in the next. That's the contrariness of the unhealthy narcissist, and that is where this book ends.

My Teachers & Selected Reading:

"When you get to the top of the mountain, keep climbing"
- Zen proverb

Buddha: The Four Noble Truths, The Noble Eightfold Path

Castaneda, Carlos: The Teachings of Don Juan: A Yaqui Way of Knowledge, Separate Reality, Journey to Ixtlan, and Tales of Power.

Fromm, Erich: To Have or To Be, The Art of Being, The Art of Loving, Escape from Freedom

Hesse, Hermann: Demian, Siddhartha, Narcissus and Goldman, Journey to the East, The Glass Bead Game

Jung, Carl: The Red Book

Maslow, Abraham: Toward A Psychology of Being

May, Rollo: Man's Search for Himself

Serrano, Miguel: C.G. Jung and Hermann Hesse: A Record of Two Friendships

Lao-Tzu: Tao-Te-Ching

Watts, Alan: Cloud-hidden - Whereabouts Unknown: A Mountain Journal,

The Joyous Cosmology - Adventures in the Chemistry of Consciousness, This Is It and Other Essays on Zen and Spiritual Experience, Wisdom of Insecurity, The Way of Zen, The Way of Tao,

Woolf, Virginia: Moments of Being

Resources for Further Reading:

Bernstein, Albert. *Emotional Vampires: Dealing With People Who Drain You Dry*. McGraw-Hill; 1 edition, (March 22, 2002).

Bradley, Ann. *Divorce: The Real Truth, the Hidden Dangers: Surviving Deception, Betrayal and Narcissism*. Amazon Digital Services; Kindle Edition.

Brown, Nina, *Children of the Self-Absorbed: A Grown-Up's Guide to Getting over Narcissistic Parents*. New Harbinger Publications; 2nd edition,(April 2008).

Brown, Nina W. *The Destructive Narcissistic Pattern*. Praeger Publishers, (August 30, 1998).

Bradshaw, John. *Healing the Shame that Binds You*. HCI; Revised edition (October 15, 2005).

Carroll, Lewis. *Alice's Adventures in Wonderland and Through the Looking Glass*. Signet Classics, (December 12, 2000).

Carnes, Patrick J. *The Betrayal Bond: Breaking Free of Exploitive Relationships*. HCI (November 1, 1997).

Carter, Les. *Enough About You, Let's Talk About Me: How to Recognize and Manage the Narcissists in Your Life*. Jossey-Bass; (January 18, 2008).

Carter, Les. *When Pleasing You Is Killing Me*. B&H Publishing Group; Workbook edition, (August 2007).

Emundson, M. (2001). *I'm OK., and then some: Heinz Kohut made his career by elaborating Freud's idea of narcissism*. Available Internet: (April 21, 2005). (http://www.nytimes.com/books/01/06/03/reviews/010603.03ed mundt.html)

Engel, Beverly. *The Emotionally Abused Woman: Overcoming Destructive Patterns and Reclaiming Yourself*. Ballantine Books. January 21, 1992

Farmer, Steven. *Adult Children of Abusive Parents: A Healing Program for Those Who Have Been Physically, Sexually, or Emotionally Abused*. Ballantine Books, (April 14, 1990).

Fiscalini, John/ Grey, Alan L. *Narcissism and the Interpersonal Self*. Columbia University Press, (April 15, 1993).

Goble, Frank G. *The Third Force: The Psychology of Abraham Maslow* (out of print).

Gonen, Jay Y. *The Roots of Nazi Psychology*. University Press of Kentucky; 2 Sub edition, (May 19, 2003).

Hotchkiss, Sandy. *Why Is It Always About You? : The Seven Deadly Sins of Narcissism*. Free Press, (August 7, 2003).

Jacoby, Mario. *Individuation and Narcissism: the Psychology of Self in Jung and Kohut*, Routledge, (March 1990).

Martinez-Lewi, Linda (PhD.) Freeing Yourself from the Narcissist in Your Life. Tarcher, (January 10, 2008).

Montagu, Ashley. Growing Young. Bergin & Garvey Paperback; 2 edition, (December 30, 1988).

Miller, Alice. The Drama of the Gifted Child: the Search for the True Self. Basic Books, (1997).

Payson, Eleanor. The Wizard of Oz and Other Narcissists: Coping with the One-Way Relationship in Work, Love, and Family. Julian Day Publications, (October 2002).

Ronningstam, Elsa. Disorders of Narcissism. American Psychiatric Publishing, Inc.; 1 edition, (January 15, 1998).

Siegel, Allen. Heinz Kohut and the Psychology of the Self: Makers of Modern Psychotherapy. Routledge(November 6, 1996).

Simon, George K. Jr. In Sheep's Clothing: Understanding and Dealing with Manipulative People. A. J. Christopher & Company, (December 19, 1996).

Stern DN. The Interpersonal World of the Infant. New York Basic Books, (1985).

Strozier, C. B. (2005). Heinz Kohut Available Internet: (April 21, 2005).
(http://www.psychologyoftheself.com/kohut /strozier1.htm)

Ver Eecke, Wilfried. Denial, Negation and the Forces of the Negative: Freud, Hegel, Lacan, Spitz, and Sophocles. SUNY Press,(2006).

Westen, Drew. Self and Society: Narcissism, Collectivism, and the Development of Morals. Cambridge University Press, (October 31, 1985).

Web Resources:

Alice Miller: Child Abuse and Mistreatment
http://www.alice-miller.com/index_en.php

Brainwashing Techniques: How Abusers Brainwash Their Victims
http://www.heart-2-heart.ca/men/page3.html

Eight Ways to Spot Emotional Manipulation
http://www.cassiopaea.com/cassiopaea/emotional_manipulation.htm

Family Violence Prevention Fund
http://endabuse.org/

Hypervigilance and Anxiety
http://www.help4trauma.org/hypervigilance.html

Information of Domestic Abuse
http://www.cwsor.org/info.htm

Liberation Psychology
http://www.mtoomey.com/breakingfree.html

Heinz Kohut
http://en.wikipedia.org/wiki/Heinz_Kohut

Narcissism 101
http://www.narcissism101.com/

Mental Disorder Network
http://www.narcissistic-personality-disorder.net/

Narcissistic Abuse
http://www.narcissisticabuse.com/

Narcissism Abuse Recovery
http://www.narcissism-abuse-recovery.com/

Narcissistic Personality Disorder (This book is dedicated to Joanna Ashmun)
http://www.halcyon.com/jmashmun/npd/

Projection of the Shadow
http://www.kheper.net/topics/psychology/projection_of_the_shadow.html

Self-Empowerment Through Setting Personal Boundaries
http://www.heart-2-heart.ca/men/page14.html

The Shadow
http://www.btinternet.com/~seamaid/shadow.htm

The Shadow Dance: Understanding Repetitive Patterns in Relationships
http://www.shadowdance.com/shadow/theshadow.html

Signs of Emotional Abuse
http://abuse101.com/emotionalabuse.html

Take Back Your Heart
http://www.takebackyourheart.com/

Ted Bundy & O.J. Simpson: Two Of A Kind
http://www.9types.com/movieboard/messages/4295.html

Voicelessness and Emotional Survival
http://www.voicelessness.com/narcissism.html

Many thanks to Wikipedia for information & excerpts on: ASD, Acquired Situational Narcissism, Erich Fromm, Hermann Hesse, Idealization and Devaluation, Individuation, Carl J. Jung, Heinz Kohut, Abraham Maslow, Hierarchy of Needs, Magical Thinking, NPD, Narcissistic Personality Disorder, Narcissistic Rage, Perfectionism, Shadow Psychology, and Wishful Thinking.

BOOK DESIGN BY E.A. DEUBLE

While the author has made every effort to provide accurate Internet addresses and reference information at the time of publication, neither the publisher nor the author assumes any responsibility for errors, or for changes that occur after publication. Further, the publisher does not have any control over and does not assume any responsibility for author or third-party websites or their content.

ISBN 0-982724829-X

CPSIA information can be obtained at www.ICGtesting.com
228830LV00006B/74/P

9 780982 724828